P9-DNU-775

1817
THE
NORMAN WILLIAMS
PUBLIC LIBRARY.
WOODSTOCK · VERMONT
DISCARD
Norman Williams Public Library
Woodstock, VT
Date May 1999
AMERICAN BANK NOTE CO NY

VOGUE KNITTING

# BABY KNITS

VOGUE KNITTING

# BABY KNITS

THE BUTTERICK® PUBLISHING COMPANY
NEW YORK

THE BUTTERICK® PUBLISHING COMPANY
161 Avenue of the Americas
New York, New York 10013



Manufactured in the United States of America

1 3 5 7 9 10 8 6 4 2

Library of Congress Card Catalog Number: 97-077517

ISBN 1-57389-011-1

First Edition

# TABLE OF CONTENTS

# INTRODUCTION

Babies and knitting are a perfect match. After all, how many people were inspired to pick up their first pair of needles to create something beautiful for the new baby in their lives? With these tiny treasures, it's easier than you think to find knitting time in a hectic schedule. Purl away your morning commute (and enjoy the "oh-it's-so-cute" comments from your fellow passengers), knit during intermission, slip in a stitch or two between meetings. Like all the projects in the *Knitting on the Go* series, baby knits are perfect for spare moments. Compact pieces—small in scale, big in creative outlet—that you can take along with you.

What could be more portable than a baby sweater? They take up little space, require a minimal investment of time and materials, and their small size makes them perfect for experimenting with stitch patterns and color combinations that might seem overwhelming in an adult-size sweater.

Better yet, these projects are fun to make. Whether you're knitting for your own child or someone else's, there's a design (or two, or three) on the pages in this book sure to delight every little one—not to mention the grown-ups. Use the yarns suggested in this book as a starting point and let your creativity soar. Search your stash for suitable odds and ends or take the plunge and splurge on a ball or two of something truly gorgeous. Experiment with fiber, color and texture (just be sure to make a test swatch for gauge) and stitch up a little style.

Pick a project, pull out your needles and get ready to KNIT ON THE GO!

# THE BASICS

For the first-time knitter or the accomplished expert, a baby sweater is one of the simplest and most expressive knitting projects. The designers who contributed to this book have created a wealth of unique and inspirational styles to choose from. Whether you knit for your own baby or as a gift for a friend, you are sure to find great pleasure in making these sweaters.

### SIZING

Most of the garments in this book are written for sizes 6 months through 24 months, with extra ease for your child to grow into the sweater. You will notice a big jump in sleeve length from size 18 months to 24 months. This is because the 24-month size is a transition from baby sizes to toddler sizes. Since children's measurements change so rapidly, it is best to measure your child or a sweater that fits them well to determine which size to make.

### YARN SELECTION

For an exact reproduction of the projects photographed, use the yarn listed in the materials section of the pattern. We've chosen yarns that are readily available in the U.S. and Canada at the time of printing. The Resources list on pages 94 and 95 provides addresses of yarn distributors. Contact them for the name of a retailer in your area.

### YARN SUBSTITUTION

You may wish to substitute yarns. Perhaps you view small-scale projects as a chance to incorporate leftovers from your yarn stash, or the yarn specified may not be available in your area. You'll need to knit to the given gauge to obtain the knitted measurements with a substitute yarn (see "Gauge" on page 11). Be sure to consider how the fiber content of the substitute yarn will affect the comfort and the ease of care of your projects.

To facilitate yarn substitution, *Vogue Knitting* grades yarn by the standard stitch gauge obtained in Stockinette stitch. You'll find a grading number in the "Materials" section of the pattern, immediately following the fiber type of the yarn. Look for a substitute yarn that falls into the same category. The suggested gauge on the ball band should be comparable to that on the "Yarn Symbols" chart on page 12.

After you've successfully gauge-swatched a substitute yarn, you'll need to figure out how much of the substitute yarn the project requires. First, find the total length of the original yarn in the pattern (multiply number of balls by yards/meters per ball). Divide this figure by the new yards/meters per ball (listed on the ball band). Round up to the next whole number. The answer is the number of balls required.

### FOLLOWING CHARTS

Charts are a convenient way to follow colorwork, lace, cable and other stitch patterns at a glance. *Vogue Knitting* stitch charts utilize the universal knitting language of "symbolcraft." When knitting in the round, read charts from right to left on every round, repeating any stitch and row repeats as directed in the pattern. When knitting back and forth in rows, read charts from right to left on right side (RS) rows and from left to right on wrong side (WS) rows. Posting a self-adhe-

## GAUGE

It is always important to knit a gauge swatch, and it is even more so with garments or they will not fit properly. If your gauge is too loose, you could end up with an over-sized garment, if it's too tight, the garment will be too small.

Patterns usually state gauge over a 4"/10cm span, however it's beneficial to make a larger test swatch. This gives a more precise stitch gauge, a better idea of the appearance and drape of the knitted fabric, and gives you a chance to familiarize yourself with the stitch pattern.

The type of needles used—straight or double pointed, wood or metal—will influence gauge, so knit your swatch with the needles you plan to use for the project. Measure gauge as illustrated. Try different needle sizes until your sample measures the required number of stitches and rows. *To get fewer stitches to the inch/cm, use larger needles; to get more stitches to the inch/cm, use smaller needles.*

Knitting in the round may tighten the gauge, so if you measured the gauge on a flat swatch, take another gauge reading after you begin knitting. When the piece measures at least 2"/5cm, lay it flat and measure over the stitches in the center of the piece, as the side stitches may be distorted.

It's a good idea to keep your gauge swatch in order to test blocking and cleaning methods.

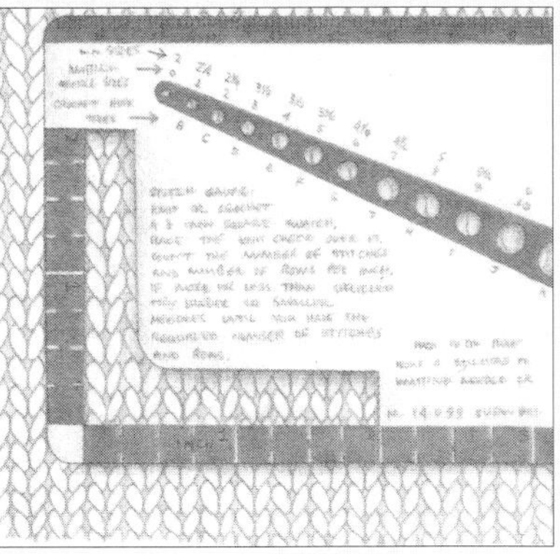

sive note under your working row is an easy way to keep track of your place on a chart.

### COLORWORK KNITTING

Two main types of colorwork are explored in this book.

### Intarsia

Intarsia is accomplished with separate bobbins of individual colors. This method is ideal for large blocks of color or for motifs that aren't repeated close together, such as the Rocking-Horse Cardigan on page 50. When changing colors, always pick up the new color and wrap it around the old color to prevent holes.

For smaller areas of color, such as the accent colors on the Fair Isle Cardigans on page 30, duplicate stitch embroidery is done after the pieces are knit.

### Stranding

When motifs are closely placed, colorwork is accomplished by stranding along two or more colors per row, creating "floats" on the wrong side of the fabric. This technique is sometimes called Fair Isle knitting, after the traditional Fair Isle patterns composed of small motifs with frequent color changes.

## BLOCKING

Blocking is an all-important finishing step in the knitting process. Most garments retain their shape after pressing if the blocking stages in the instructions are followed carefully.

### WET BLOCK METHOD

Using rust-proof pins, pin pieces to measurements on a flat surface and lightly dampen using a spray bottle. Allow to dry before removing pins.

### STEAM BLOCK METHOD

With WS facing, pin pieces to measurements. Steam lightly, holding the iron 2"/5cm above the knitting. Do not press, as it will flatten stitches.

#### TO BEGIN SEAMING

If you have left a long tail from your cast-on row, you can use this strand to begin sewing. To make a neat join at the lower edge with no gap, use the technique shown here. Thread the strand into a tapestry needle. With the right sides of both pieces facing you, insert the tapestry needle from back to front into the corner stitch of the piece without the tail. Making a figure eight with the yarn, insert the needle from back to front into the stitch with the cast-on tail. Tighten to close the gap.

#### INVISIBLE SEAMING: STOCKINETTE STITCH

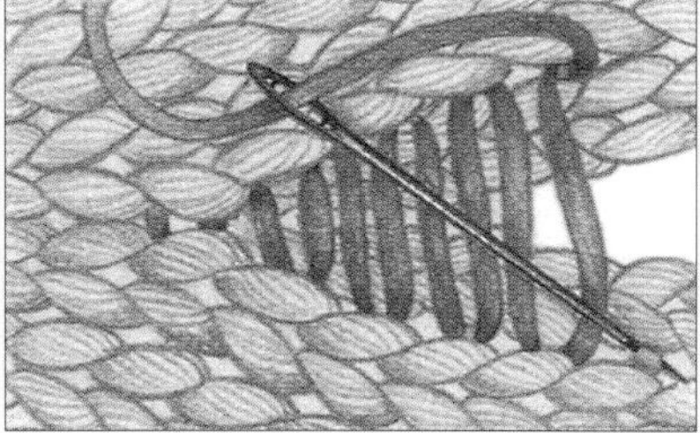

To make an invisible side seam in a garment worked in stockinette stitch, insert the tapestry needle under the horizontal bar between the first and second stitches. Insert the needle into the corresponding bar on the other piece. Pull the yarn gently until the sides meet. Continue alternating from side to side.

#### YARN SYMBOLS

**① Fine Weight**
(29-32 stitches per 4"/10cm)
*Includes baby and fingering yarns, and some of the heavier crochet cottons. The range of needle sizes is 0-4 (2-3.5mm).*

**② Lightweight**
(25-28 stitches per 4"/10cm)
*Includes sport yarn, sock yarn, UK 4-ply and lightweight DK yarns. The range of needle sizes is 3-6 (3.25-4mm).*

**③ Medium Weight**
(21-24 stitches per 4"/10cm)
*Includes DK and worsted, the most commonly used knitting yarns. The range of needle sizes is 6-9 (4-5.5mm).*

**④ Medium-heavy Weight**
(17-20 stitches per 4"/10cm)
*Also called heavy worsted or Aran. The range of needle sizes is 8-10 (5-6mm).*

**⑤ Bulky Weight**
(13-16 stitches per 4"/10cm)
*Also called chunky. Includes heavier Icelandic yarns. The range of needle sizes is 10-11 (6-8mm).*

**⑥ Extra-bulky Weight**
(9-12 stitches per 4"/10cm)
*The heaviest yarns available. The range of needle sizes is 11 and up (8mm and up).*

# KNITTING TERMS AND ABBREVIATIONS

**approx** approximately

**beg** begin(ning)

**bind off** Used to finish an edge and keep stitches from unraveling. Lift second over the third, etc. (UK: cast off)

**cast on** A foundation row of stitches placed on the needle in order to begin knitting.

**CC** contrast color

**ch** chain(s)

**cm** centimeter(s)

**cont** continu(e)(ing)

**dec** decrease(ing)—Reduce the stitches in a row (knit 2 together).

**dpn** double pointed needle(s)

**foll** follow(s)(ing)

**g** gram(s)

**garter stitch** Knit every row. Circular knitting: knit one round, then purl one round.

**inc** increase(ing)—Add stitches in a row (knit into the front and back of a stitch).

**k** knit

**k2tog** knit 2 stitches together

**LH** left-hand

**lp(s)** loops(s)

**m** meter(s)

**M1** make one stitch—With the needle tip, lift the strand between last stitch worked and next stitch on the left-hand needle and knit into the back of it. One stitch has been added.

**MC** main color

**mm** millimeter(s)

**oz** ounce(s)

**p** purl

**p2tog** purl 2 stitches together

**pat(s)** pattern

**pick up and knit (purl)** Knit (or purl) into the loops along an edge.

**pm** place markers—Place or attach a loop of contrast yarn or purchased stitch marker as indicated.

**psso** pass slip stitch(es) over

**rem** remain(s)(ing)

**rep** repeat

**rev St st** reverse Stockinette stitch—Purl right-side rows, knit wrong-side rows. Circular knitting: purl all rounds. (UK: reverse stocking stitch)

**rnd(s)** round(s)

**RH** right-hand

**RS** right side(s)

**sc** single crochet (UK: dc—double crochet)

**sk** skip

**SKP** Slip 1, knit 1, pass slip stitch over knit 1.

**SK2P** Slip 1, knit 2 together, pass slip stitch over the knit 2 together.

**sl** slip-An unworked stitch made by passing a stitch from the left-hand to the right-hand needle as if to purl.

**sl st** slip stitch (UK: single crochet)

**ssk** slip, slip, knit—Slip next 2 stitches knitwise, one at a time, to right-hand needle. Insert tip of left-hand needle into fronts of these stitches from left to right. Knit them together. One stitch has been decreased.

**sssk** Slip next 3 sts knitwise, one at a time, to right-hand needle. Insert tip of left-hand needle into fronts of these stitches from left to right. Knit them together. Two stitches have been decreased.

**st(s)** stitch(es)

**St st** Stockinette stitch—Knit right-side rows, purl wrong-side rows. Circular knitting: knit all rounds. (UK: stocking stitch)

**tbl** through back of loop

**tog** together

**WS** wrong side(s)

**wyib** with yarn in back

**wyif** with yarn in front

**yd** yard(s)

**yo** yarn over—Make a new stitch by wrapping the yarn over the right-hand needle. (UK: yfwd, yon, yrn)

*** =** Repeat directions following * as many times as indicated.

**[ ] =** Repeat directions inside brackets as many times as indicated.

# SAILBOAT CARDIGAN

*Anchors aweigh!*

*For Intermediate Knitters*

**Set sail for adventure with this easy-to-knit cardigan. Tiny felt flags top each sailboat; striped sleeves complete the nautical look. Designed by Amy Bahrt.**

### SIZES

Instructions are written for size 3 months. Changes for sizes 6, 12, 18 and 24 months are in parentheses.

### KNITTED MEASUREMENTS

- Chest 21¾ (23, 24¾, 26, 27)"/55.5 (58.5, 63, 66, 68.5)cm
- Length 9½ (10½, 11½, 12½, 14)"/24 (26.5, 29, 32, 35.5)cm
- Upper arm 9 (9½, 10, 10½, 11½)"/23 (24, 25, 26.5, 29)cm

### MATERIALS

- 2 (2, 2, 3, 3) 3½oz/100g balls (each approx 185yd/170m) of Reynolds *Saucy* (cotton④) in #292 blue (A)
- 1 ball each in #130 yellow (B), #800 white (C), and #529 green (D)
- One pair each sizes 5 and 7 (3.75 and 4.5 mm) needles *or size to obtain gauge*
- 3 stitch holders
- Small piece of washable yellow felt
- Tapestry needle
- 4 (4, 4, 5, 5) ½"/13mm buttons

### GAUGE

20 sts and 26 rows to 4"/10cm over St st using larger needles.
*Take time to check gauge.*

**Note** When changing colors, twist yarns on WS to prevent holes in work.

### STRIPE PATTERN

Work in St st as foll: *4 rows A, 2 rows B; rep from * (6 rows) for stripe pat.

### BACK

With smaller needles and B, cast on 51 (55, 59, 63, 65) sts. Work in k1, p1 rib for 1"/2.5cm, end with a WS row.
Change to larger needles and work in St st for 4 rows C.

#### Beg chart I

**Row 1 (RS)** Beg with st 1 (5, 3, 1, 1), work to st 6, work 6-st rep 7 (8, 9, 9, 9) times, work first 3 (5, 1, 3, 5) sts once more. Cont as established through chart row 2. With A, work 4 rows even.

#### Beg chart II

**Row 1 (RS)** K2 (4, 6, 8, 9) A, [work 13 sts chart II, k4 A] twice, work 13 sts chart II, k2 (4, 6, 8, 9) A.
Cont as established through row 10. Cont with A only until piece measures 9½ (10½, 11½, 12½, 14)"/24 (26.5, 29, 32, 35.5)cm from beg, end with a WS row.
**Next row** Bind off 16 (17, 19, 20, 21) sts, work center 19 (21, 21, 23, 23) sts and place on holder for back neck, bind off rem sts.

### LEFT FRONT

With smaller needles and B, cast on 25 (27, 29, 31, 33) sts. Work in k1, p1 rib as for back, inc 1 (1, 1, 0, 0) st on last WS row—26 (28, 30, 31, 33) sts. Change to larger needles and work in St st for 4 rows C.

#### Beg chart I

**Row 1 (RS)** Beg with st 1 (5, 3, 1, 1), work to st 6, work 6-st rep 3 (4, 4, 4, 4) times, work first 2 (2, 2, 1, 3) sts once. Cont as established through chart row 2. With A, work 4 rows even.

#### Beg chart II

**Row 1 (RS)** K7 (8, 9, 9, 10) A, work 13 sts chart II, k6 (7, 8, 9, 10) A. Cont as established through row 10. Then cont with A only until piece measures 7 (8, 9, 10,

11½)"/17.5 (20, 22.5, 25.5, 29)cm from beg, end with a RS row.

**Neck shaping**

**Next row (WS)** Bind off 4 (5, 5, 5, 5) sts, work to end. Cont to bind off from neck edge 2 sts twice, then dec 1 st every other row 2 (2, 2, 2, 3) times—16 (17, 19, 20, 21) sts. Work even until same length as back to shoulder. Bind off.

## RIGHT FRONT

Work as for left front, reversing chart placement and neck shaping.

## SLEEVES

With smaller needles and B, cast on 31 (31, 33, 33, 35) sts. Work in k1, p1 rib for 1"/2.5cm, inc 4 (5, 5, 6, 5) sts evenly across last WS row—35 (36, 38, 39, 40) sts. Change to larger needles and work in St st for 2 rows C.

**Beg chart I**

**Row I (RS)** Beg at st 1 (1, 6, 5, 5), work to st 6, work 6-st rep 4 (5, 6, 6, 6) times, work first 5 (0, 0, 1, 2) sts once. Cont as established through chart row 2. Work in St st and stripe pat, inc 1 st each side every 4th (6th, 6th, 6th, 8th) row 5 (6, 6, 7, 9) times—45 (48, 50, 53, 58) sts. Work even until piece measures 5½ (6, 6½, 7¾, 11½)"/14 (15.5, 16.5, 19.5, 29)cm from beg, end with a WS row. Bind off.

## FINISHING

Foll template, cut 5 yellow felt flags and sew each to top of sailboat, pointing right. Sew shoulder seams.

**Neckband**

With RS facing, smaller needles and B, pick up and k 55 (57, 57, 61, 61) sts evenly around neck edge, including back neck sts on holder. Work in k1, p1 rib for 1"/2.5cm. Bind off.

**Buttonband**

**Note** Work on left side for girls, on right side for boys.

With RS facing, smaller needles and B, pick up and k 47 (53, 59, 65, 73) sts evenly along front edge. Complete as for neckband. Place markers on band for 4 (4, 4, 5, 5) buttons, the first and last ones at ½"/1.5cm from edges and the others spaced evenly between.

**Buttonhole band**

Work as for buttonband on opposite front edge for ½"/1.5cm, end with a WS row. Work buttonholes on next row opposite markers by binding off 2 sts for each buttonhole. On next row, cast on 2 sts over bound-off sts. Complete as for buttonband. Place markers 4½ (4¾, 5, 5¼, 5¾)"/11.5 (12, 12.5, 13.5, 14.5)cm down from shoulders on front and back. Sew sleeves between markers. Sew side and sleeve seams. Sew on buttons.

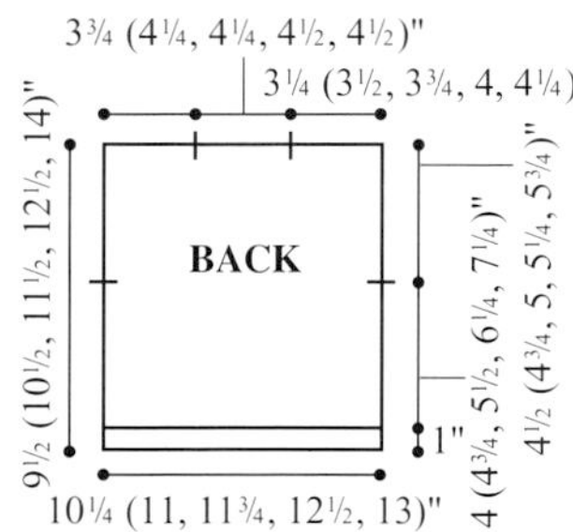


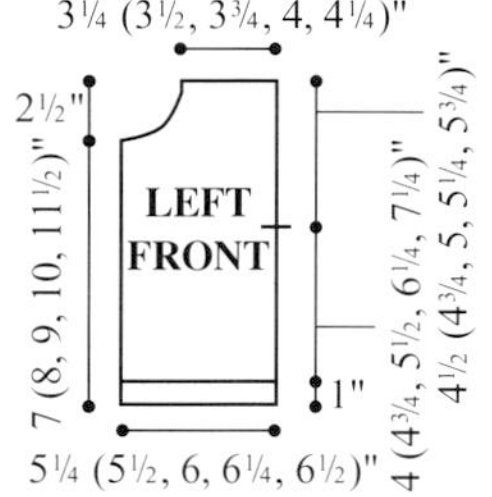


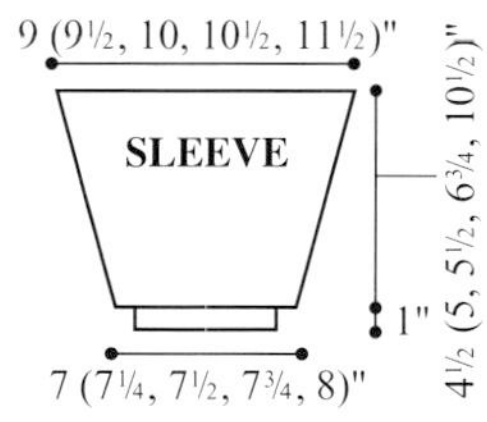


## FLAG TEMPLATE

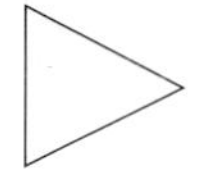

**Color key**

Blue (A)

White (C)

Green (D)

## CHART I

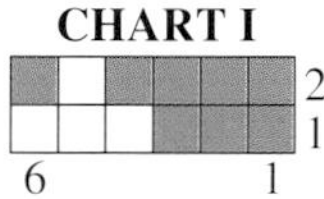


## CHART II

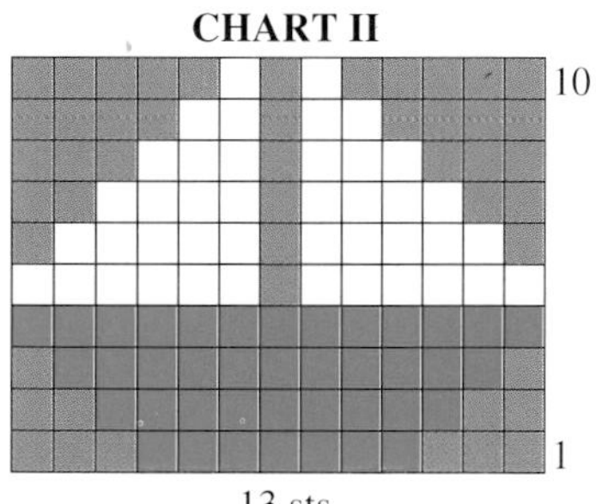

# PLAY SET

*Show your stripes*

**Cute two-piece features a hooded top and patch pocket; the pants have a wide elastic waist. Seed-stitch edges and a mix of colorful stripes make it extra special. Designed by Gitta Schrade.**

## SIZES

Instructions are written for size 6 months. Changes for sizes 12, 18 and 24 months are in parentheses.

## KNITTED MEASUREMENTS

### Pullover

- Chest 22 (24, 26, 28)"/56 (61, 66, 71)cm
- Length 11 (12, 13, 14)"/28 (30.5, 33, 33.5)cm
- Upper arm 9½ (10, 11, 12)"/24 (25.5, 28, 31)cm

### Pants

- Hip 23½ (24, 26, 28)"/59 (60, 65, 71)cm
- Length 10½ (11½, 12½, 13½)"/26.5 (29, 31.5, 34)cm

## MATERIALS

- 3 (4, 4, 4) 2½oz/70g balls (each approx 168yd/154m) of Lion Brand *Micro Spun* (acrylic③) in #144 lilac (MC)
- 2 (2, 2, 2) balls in #100 white (A)
- 1 (1, 2, 2) balls in #146 fuchsia (B)
- One pair each sizes 2 and 4 (2.5 and 3.5mm) needles *or size to obtain gauge*
- Size D/3 (3mm) crochet hook
- Stitch markers and holders

### Pants

- Size 2 (2.5mm) circular needle, 16"/40cm long
- 1yd/1m of 1"/2.5cm elastic
- Tapestry needle

## GAUGE

23 sts and 34 rows to 4"/10 cm over St st using larger needles.
*Take time to check gauge.*

## STITCH GLOSSARY

### Seed stitch

**Row 1 (RS)** *K1, p1; rep from * to end.
**Row 2** K the purl sts and p the knit sts.
Rep row 2 for seed st.

### Stripe Pattern I

*4 rows A, 4 rows MC; rep from * (8 rows) for stripe I.

### Stripe Pattern II

*4 rows B, 4 rows MC; rep from * (8 rows) for stripe II.

## PULLOVER

## BACK

With smaller needles and MC, cast on 68 (74, 80, 86) sts. Work in seed st for 4 rows, inc 1 st on last row—69 (75, 81, 87) sts. Change to larger needles and work in St st and stripe pat I, dec 1 st each side every 14th (16th, 18th, 20th) row 3 times—63 (69, 75, 81) sts. Work even until piece measures 11 (12, 13, 14)"/28 (30.5, 33, 35.5)cm from beg, end with a WS row. Bind off all sts.

## FRONT

Work as for back until piece measures 9¼ (10, 10¾, 11½)"/23.5 (25.5, 27, 29)cm from beg, end with a WS row.

### Neck shaping

**Next row (RS)** Work 25 (27, 30, 32) sts, join 2nd ball and bind off center 25 (27, 30, 32) sts, work to end. Working both sides at once, bind off from each neck edge 3 sts once, 2 sts once, dec 1 st every other row 3 times. Work even until same length as back. Bind off rem 17 (19, 22, 24) sts each side for shoulders.

### SLEEVES

With smaller needles and MC, cast on 38 (40, 40, 42) sts. Work in seed st for 4 rows, inc 1 st on last row—39 (41, 41, 43) sts. Change to larger needles and work in St st and stripe pat II, inc 1 st each side every 4th row 5 (2, 7, 0) times, every 6th row 3 (6, 4, 13) times—55 (57, 63, 69) sts. Work even until piece measures 6 (6½, 7½, 11)"/15.5 (16.5, 19, 28)cm from beg. Bind off all sts.

### HOOD

With larger needles and MC, cast on 37 (39, 42, 45) sts. Work in St st and stripe pat I, inc 1 st at beg of every RS row 3 (2, 0, 9) times, then at beg of every other RS row 9 (10, 12, 12) times—49 (51, 54, 57) sts. Work even until piece measures 9½ (9¾, 10, 10½)"/24 (25, 25.5, 26.5)cm from beg. Place marker at beg and end of row. Work 2nd half of hood to correspond to first half, working decs instead of incs—37 (39, 42, 45) sts. Bind off.

### POCKET

With smaller needles and B, cast on 26 (26, 32, 35) sts. Work in seed st for 4 rows. Change to larger needles and work in St st until piece measures 2 (2, 2¼, 2½)"/5 (5, 6, 6.5)cm from beg, end with a WS row. Bind off 3 sts at beg next 4 rows, 2 (2, 3, 3) sts at beg next 2 rows, 2 sts at beg next 2 rows. Bind off rem 6 (6, 10, 13) sts.

### FINISHING

Block pieces. Sew shoulder seams. Place markers 4¾ (5, 5½, 6)"/12 (12.5, 14, 15.5)cm down from shoulder seam on front and back for armhole. Sew top of sleeves between markers. Sew side and sleeve seams.

**Pocket edging**

With RS facing, crochet hook and B, work sc along sides and shaped edge, inserting hook through the back of each edge st, turn at end.

**Row 2** Work sc in each sc. Fasten off. Sew pocket to front (see photo for placement).

**Hood edging**

With RS facing, smaller needles and MC, pick up and k 162 (166, 170, 170) sts evenly around hood. Work in St st for ½"/1.5cm. Bind off. Fold edging to WS of hood and sew in place

### PANTS

### RIGHT HALF

Beg at bottom of leg, with smaller needles and MC, cast on 60 (66, 72, 78) sts. Work in seed st for 4 rows. Change to larger needles and work in St st and stripe pat II as foll:

Inc 1 st each side every other row 5 (3, 3, 1) times, every 4th row 3 (5, 6, 8) times—76 (82, 90, 96) sts. Work even until piece measures 3½ (4, 4½, 5)"/9 (10, 11.5, 12.5)cm from beg, end with a WS row. Bind off 3 sts at beg of next 2 rows.

**Next row (RS)** Bind off 1 (1, 2, 2) sts, work to end.

**Next row (WS)** Bind off 2 sts, work to end. Dec 1 st at beg of next 2 rows.

**Next row (RS)** Dec 0 (0, 0, 1) st, work to end. Dec 1 st at beg of next 1 (1, 2, 3) WS rows—64 (70, 76, 80) sts. Work even until piece measures 9½ (10½, 11½, 12½)"/24 (26.5, 29, 32)cm from beg, end with a 4th row of B. Place sts on holder.

### LEFT HALF

Work to correspond to right half, but work in stripe pat I and reverse crotch shaping.

### FINISHING

## Waistband

Sew leg seams. Sew legs tog at center front and back.

With RS facing, MC and circular needle, pick up and k sts from holders—128 (140, 156, 160) sts. Join and work in k1, p1 rib for 1"/2.5cm. P next rnd for turning ridge. Cont in rib for 1"/2.5 cm more. Bind off. Fold waistband to WS at turning ridge and sew in place, leaving opening for elastic. Cut elastic to fit waist plus 1"/2.5cm. Overlap and sew ends tog and close opening.

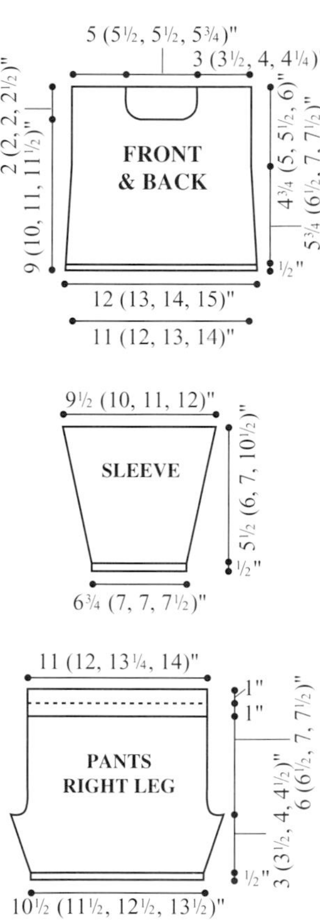

# CAR JACKET AND HAT

*Start your engines!*

*For Intermediate Knitters*

**Colorful cars hit the road on this cozy jacket with front pockets to keep little hands warm. More cars circle the matching cap; a plump pom-pom tops it off. Designed by Sasha Kagan.**

### SIZES

#### Cardigan

Instructions are written for size 6 months. Changes for sizes 12, 18 and 24 months are in parentheses.

#### Hat

Instructions are written for size 6-12 months. Changes for size 18-24 months are in parentheses.

### KNITTED MEASUREMENTS

#### Cardigan

- Chest (buttoned) 22½ (24½, 25½, 26¾)"/57 (62, 64.5, 68)cm
- Length 10½ (11, 12, 14)"/26.5 (28, 30.5, 35.5)cm
- Upper arm 10 (11, 12, 13)"/25 (28, 31, 33)cm

#### Hat

- Head circumference 16½ (17¼)"/42 (43.5)cm

### MATERIALS

- 4 (5, 5, 6) .8oz/25g balls (approx 75d/67m) of Rowan *Lightweight DK* (wool②) in #62 black (A)
- 2 (2, 3, 3) balls in #65 grey (B)
- 1 ball each in #614 beige (C), #618 orange (D), #124 green (E), #126 purple (F), #50 pale blue (G), #75 lime (H), and #45 brick (I)
- One pair each sizes 3 and 5 (3 and 3.75mm) needles *or size to obtain gauge*
- 2 stitch holders
- Tapestry needle
- 6 (6, 6, 7) ½"/13mm car buttons

### GAUGE

26 sts and 32 rows to 4"/10cm over St st and car chart, using larger needles.
*Take time to check gauge.*

#### Notes

**1)** When changing colors, twist yarns on WS to prevent holes in work.
**2)** Use bobbins for each car and carry background color at back of work.
**3)** Duplicate st small color areas if desired.

### RIB PATTERN

(multiple of 4 sts plus 2)
**Row 1 (RS)** K2 A, *p2 B, k2 A; rep from * to end.
**Row 2** P2 A, *k2 B, p2 A; rep from * to end.
Rep rows 1 and 2 for rib pat.

### BACK

With smaller needles and A, cast on 70 (78, 82, 86) sts. Work in rib pat for 1½"/4cm, inc 2 (0, 0, 0) sts on last WS row—72 (78, 82, 86) sts. Change to larger needles and work in St st for 0 (0, ½, 1)"/0 (0, 1.5, 2.5)cm with A, end with a WS row.

#### Beg car chart

**Row 1 (RS)** Beg with st 64 (61, 59, 57) work to st 66, work sts 1-66 once, then work first 3 (6, 8, 10) sts once more. Cont in chart as established until 34 rows of chart have been worked twice. With A, work in St st until piece measures 10 (10½, 11½, 13½)"/25 (26.5, 29, 34)cm, end with a WS row.

#### Shoulder shaping

Bind off 12 (13, 14, 14) sts at beg of next 2 rows, 13 (14, 14, 15) sts at beg of next 2 rows. Bind off rem 22 (24, 26, 28) sts for back neck.

### LEFT FRONT

With smaller needles and A, cast on 34 (38, 42, 42) sts. Work in rib pat for 1½"/4cm, inc 2 (inc 1, dec 1, inc 1) sts on last WS row—36 (39, 41, 43) sts. Change to larger needles.

**Beg car chart**

**Row 1 (RS)** Beg with st 64 (61, 59, 57) work to st 66, work sts 1-33 once. Cont in chart as established for 4 (6, 6, 8) rows.

**Pocket dividing**

**Next row (RS)** Working each side of pocket separately and cont in established pat, k20 (23, 25, 27) sts, turn leaving rem sts on holder. Work even for 20 (22, 24, 26) rows. Leave these sts on holder. Place 16 sts from first holder back to needle and work to match first side.

**Joining row (RS)** Work even in pat over all 36 (39, 41, 43) sts until piece measures 8¼ (8¾, 9¾, 11¾)"/21 (22.5, 25, 30)cm from beg, ending with a RS row.

**Neck shaping**

**Next row (RS)** Bind off 4 (5, 6, 7) sts (neck edge), work to end. Cont to dec 1 st at neck edge every other row 7 times—25 (27, 28, 29) sts. Work even until same length as back to shoulder. Shape shoulder at beg of RS rows as for back.

### RIGHT FRONT

Work as for left front, reversing shaping, pocket placement and chart as foll:

**Beg car chart**

**Row 1 (RS)** Beg with st 33 work to st 66, then work first 3 (6, 8, 10) sts once more.

### SLEEVES

With smaller needles and A, cast on 42 (46, 46, 50) sts. Work in rib pat for 1"/2.5cm, inc 6 (4, 6, 4) sts evenly across last WS row—48 (50, 52, 54) sts. Change larger needles and work in St st with A for 0 (1, 1½, 2)"/0 (2.5, 4, 5)cm. Cont in car chart (centering pat) for 34 rows, then cont with A only to end of piece, AT SAME TIME, inc 1 st each side every 4th row 9 (8, 11, 15) times, every other row 0 (3, 2, 0) times—66 (72, 78, 84) sts. Work even until piece measures 6 (6½, 7¾, 11)"/15.5 (16.5, 19.5, 28)cm from beg. Bind off.

### FINISHING

With tapestry needle, work Duplicate stitch with appropriate colors to complete chart if necessary. Sew shoulder seams.

**Pocket lining**

With RS facing, larger needles and A, pick up and k 15 (17, 18, 20) sts evenly along side of pocket opening nearest side edge. Beg with a purl row, work in St st for 4 (4½, 5, 5½)"/10 (11.5, 12.5, 14)cm from beg. Bind off. Fold in half with RS tog and slip st bound-off edge to other side of pocket opening. Sew side seams.

**Buttonband**

(Work on left side for girls, on right side for boys)

With RS facing, larger needles and A, pick up and k 73 (77, 85, 103) sts evenly on front edge. Work in k1, p1 rib for 4 rows. Bind off in rib. Place markers on band for 6 (6, 6, 7) buttons, the first one ¼"/1cm from lower edge, the last one ½"/1.5cm from top edge, and the others spaced evenly between.

**Buttonhole band**

Work as for buttonband on opposite front edge for 1 row. Work buttonholes on next row opposite markers by working yo, k2tog for each buttonhole. Complete as for buttonband.

**Collar**

With WS facing, larger needles and A, pick up and k 74 (78, 82, 86) sts evenly around neck edge, beg and end at center of front bands. Work 3 rows St st with A, then beg with row 2, work in rib pat for 2"/5cm. Bind off with A.

Place markers 5 (5½, 6, 6½)"/12.5 (14, 15.5, 16.5)cm down from shoulder seams on front and back for armholes. Sew top of sleeves between markers. Sew side and sleeve seams. Sew on buttons.

## HAT

With smaller needles and A, cast on 106 (110) sts. Work in rib pat for 2"/5cm, inc 2 sts on last WS row—108 (112) sts. Change to larger needles.

**Beg car chart**

**Row 1 (RS)** Rep sts 31 (30) to 66 three times, work st 0 (30) once more. Cont in pat as established through row 18, dec 0 (4) sts evenly on last row—108 sts.

Cont with B to end of piece as foll: work in St st for 2 (6) rows.

**Shape top**

**Row 1 (RS)** [K7, k2tog] 12 times—96 sts.

**Row 2 and all wrong side rows** Purl.

**Row 3** [K6, k2tog] 12 times—84 sts.

Cont in this way to dec 12 sts every RS row until 36 sts rem. P 1 row.

**Next row (RS)** K2 tog across—18 sts.

Cut yarn, leaving an end for sewing. Thread through rem sts and pull tightly to close.

## FINISHING

With tapestry needle, work Duplicate stitch with appropriate colors to complete chart if necessary. Sew back seam.

With I, make a 1½"/4cm pom-pom and attach at top of hat.

**POM-POM TEMPLATE**

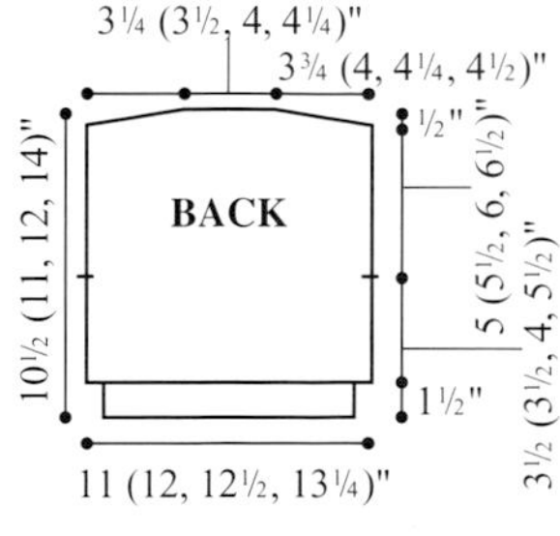


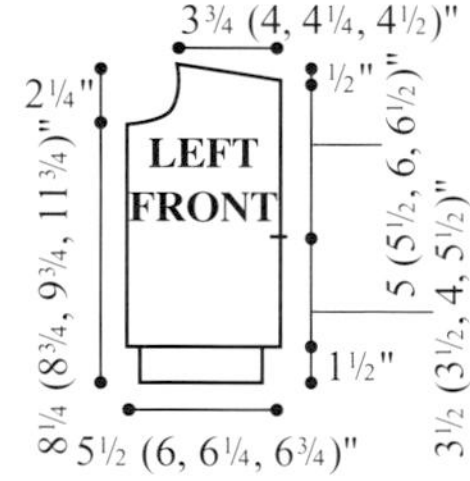


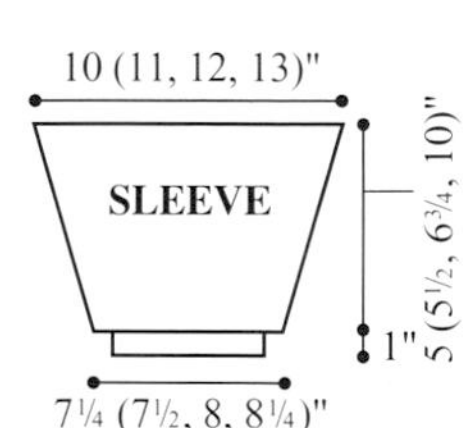

## CAR CHART

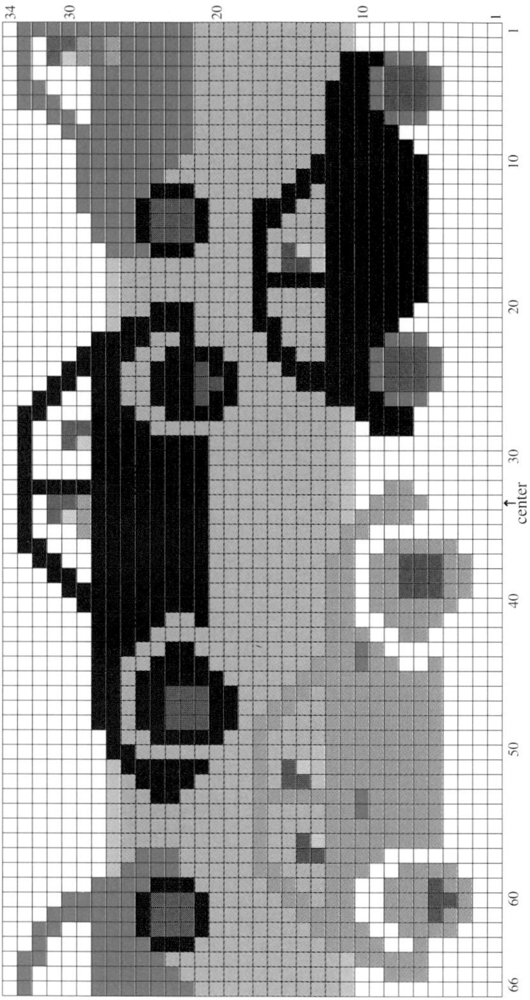

### Color key

| | | |
|---|---|---|
| Black (A) | Orange (D) | Pale Blue (G) |
| Grey (B) | Green (E) | Lime (H) |
| Beige (C) | Purple (F) | Brick (I) |

## POM-POM

**1** *Following the template, cut two circular pieces of cardboard.*

**2** *Hold the two circles together and wrap the yarn tightly around the cardboard several times. Secure and carefully cut the yarn.*

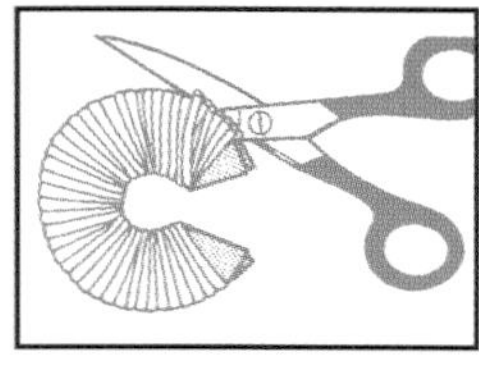

**3** *Tie a piece a yarn tightly between the two circles. Remove the cardboard and trim the pom-pom to the desired size.*

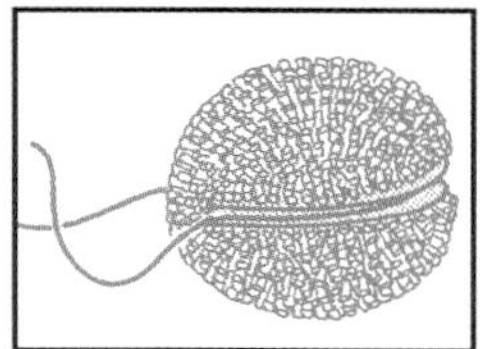

# SLIP-STITCH CARDIGAN

*Tailored texture*

**Pretty patterned cardigan contrasts variegated yarn with basic off white. The effect is created with a simple slip stitch. Seed-stitch edges and collar are a perfect frame. Designed by Abigail Liles.**

### SIZES

Instructions are written for size 6 months. Changes for sizes 12, 18 and 24 months are in parentheses.

### KNITTED MEASUREMENTS

- Chest 21 (23, 25, 26)"/53.5 (58.5, 63.5, 66)cm
- Length 10 (11, 12, 14)"/25.5 (28, 30.5, 35.5)cm
- Upper arm 8 (9, 10, 11)"/20 (23, 25, 28)cm

### MATERIALS

- 2 (3, 3, 4) 1¾oz/50g balls (each approx 107yd/98m) of Brown Sheep *Kaleidescope* (cotton/wool④) in Anaheim (MC)
- 1 (2, 2, 2) 3½oz/100g skeins (each approx 215yd/197m) of Brown Sheep *Cotton Fleece* (cotton/wool④) in #CW-100 cotton ball (CC)
- One pair each sizes 5 and 6 (3.75 and 4mm) needles *or size to obtain gauge*
- 5 (5, 5, 6) ½"/15mm buttons

### GAUGE

23 sts and 45 rows to 4"/10cm over pat st using larger needles.
*Take time to check gauge.*

### STITCH GLOSSARY

#### Pattern Stitch

(odd number of sts)
**Row 1 (RS)** With MC, knit.
**Row 2** With MC, purl.
**Row 3** With CC, k1, *sl 1 purlwise wyib, k1; rep from *, end k1.
**Row 4** With CC, k1, *sl 1 purlwise wyif, k1; rep from *, end k1.
Rep rows 1-4 for pat st.

#### Seed Stitch

**Row 1 (RS)** *K1, p1; rep from * to end.
**Row 2** K the purl sts and p the knit sts.
Rep row 2 for seed st.

### BACK

With smaller needles and CC, cast on 57 (63, 67, 71) sts. Work in seed st for 7 rows, end with a RS row. P next row on WS, inc 4 sts evenly across—61 (67, 71, 75) sts. Change to larger needles and MC. Work in pat st until piece measures 10 (11, 12, 14)"/25.5 (28, 30.5, 35.5)cm from beg. Bind off all sts.

### LEFT FRONT

With smaller needles and CC, cast on 25 (29, 31, 33) sts Work in seed st for 7 rows, end with a RS row. P next row on WS, inc 2 sts evenly across—27 (31, 33, 35) sts. Change to larger needles and MC. Work in pat st until piece measures 8 (9, 10, 12)"/20.5 (23, 25.5, 30.5)cm from beg, end with a RS row.

#### Neck shaping

**Next row (WS)** Bind off 4 (3, 4, 4) sts (neck edge), work to end. Work 3 rows even. Bind off 2 sts at neck edge on next row, then every 4th row twice more. Work even until same length as back. Bind off rem 17 (22, 23, 25) sts for shoulder.

### RIGHT FRONT

Work as for left front, reversing shaping.

### SLEEVES

With smaller needles and CC, cast on 27 (29, 29, 31) sts. Work in seed st for 7 rows, end with a RS row. P next row on WS, inc

2 sts evenly across—29 (31, 31, 33) sts. Change to larger needles and MC. Work in pat st, inc 1 st each side (working inc sts into pat) every 4th (4th, 4th, 8th) row 3 (3, 6, 9) times, every 6th row 6 (7, 7, 6) times—47 (51, 57, 63) sts. Work even until piece measures 6¼ (6¾, 7¾, 11½)"/16 (17, 19.5, 29)cm from beg. Bind off all sts.

**FINISHING**

Block pieces to measurements. Place markers 4 (4½, 5, 5½)"/10 (11.5, 12.5, 14)cm down from shoulders on front and back. Sew sleeves between markers.

**Collar**

With WS facing, smaller needles and CC, pick up and k 65 (65, 69, 69) sts evenly around neck. Work in seed st for 2"/5cm. Bind off in seed st.

**Buttonband**

With RS facing, smaller needles and CC, pick up and k 45 (51, 57, 67) sts evenly along left front. Work in seed st for 7 rows. Bind off in seed st. Place markers for 5 (5, 5, 6) buttons with the first and last one at ½"/1.5cm from upper and lower edges and 3 (3, 3, 4) others spaced evenly between.

**Buttonhole band**

With RS facing, smaller needles and CC, pick up and k 45 (51, 57, 67) sts evenly along right front. Work in seed st for 3 rows.

**Next row (RS)** Work buttonholes opposite markers as foll: k2tog, yo. Work 3 more rows. Bind off in seed st.

Sew side and sleeve seams. Sew on buttons.

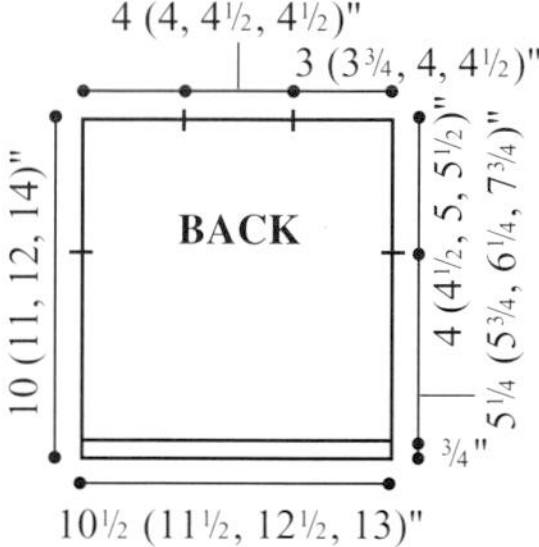


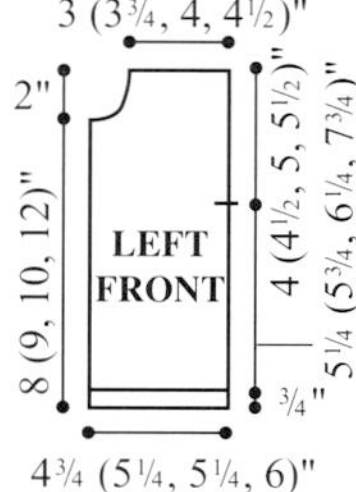

# FAIR ISLE CARDIGANS

*Crazy for color*

*For Intermediate Knitters*

**Make your choice from two versions of this adorable brightly-colored Fair Isle cardigan. Mix and match sleeves and lower bands; the corrugated ribbing offsets the colorwork. Designed by Kristin Nicholas.**

### SIZES

Instructions are written for size 6 months. Changes for sizes 12, 18 and 24 months are in parentheses.

### KNITTED MEASUREMENTS

- Chest 22 (24, 26, 28)"/56 (61, 66, 63.5)cm
- Length 10 (11, 12, 13)"/25.5 (28, 30.5, 33)cm
- Upper arm 9 (9, 10, 10)"/23 (23, 25.5, 25.5)cm

### MATERIALS

- 1¾oz/50g hanks (each approx 95yd/87m) of Classic Elite *Tapestry* (wool④)

**Floral border version**

- 2 (2, 2, 3) hanks #2231 turquoise (A)
- 2 (2, 2, 3) hanks each #2258 red (B) and #2285 mustard(C)
- 1 (1, 2, 2) hanks #2284 coral (D)
- 1 hank each #2246 teal (E) and #2272 green (F)

**Square border version**

- 1 hank each #2231 turquoise (A) and #2296 daffodil (B)
- 1 (2, 2, 2) hanks #2210 navy (C)
- 1 hank #2284 coral (D)
- 2 (2, 2, 3) hanks #2272 green (E)
- 1 (1, 1, 2) hanks #2205 pink (F)

**Both versions**

- One pair each sizes 4 and 5 (3.5 and 3.75 mm) needles *or size to obtain gauge*
- Size 4 (3.5 mm) circular needle 24"/60cm long
- Stitch holders
- Tapestry needle
- Four ¾"/20mm buttons

### GAUGE

22 sts and 24 rows to 4"/10cm over St st and Fair Isle charts using larger needles. *Take time to check gauge.*

**Notes**

**1)** Sweater is shown in two color pat versions. The first colors listed refer to floral border version, colors in [ ] refer to square border version.
**2)** Body is worked in one piece to armhole, then both fronts and back are worked separately to shoulder.
**3)** When changing colors, twist yarns on WS to prevent holes in work.
**4)** Work Duplicate st for accent color on charts I and II.

### BODY

With smaller needles and D [B], cast on 110 (122, 130, 142) sts. P 1 row, k 1 row.

**Beg rib pat**

**Row 1 (RS)** K2 F [A], *k2 C [F], k2 F [A]; rep from * to end.
**Row 2** P2 F [A], *k2 C [F], p2 F [A]; rep from * to end.
**Row 3** K2 F [A], *p2 C [F], k2 F [A]; rep from * to end.
Rep rows 2 and 3 twice more. With D [D], p 2 rows, k 1 row, inc 3 (1, 5, 3) sts evenly across last row—113 (123, 135, 145) sts. Change to larger needles and work in St st as foll:

**Beg chart I**

**Row 1 (RS)** Using appropriate chart for selected version, work sts 10 (10, 9-10, 9-

10), work sts 1-10 to last 2 (2, 3, 3) sts, then work sts 1-2 (1-2, 1-3, 1-3). Cont as established through row 12. With D [D], k 2 rows, p 2 rows. Cont in St st, work rows 1-16 of chart II for selected version for rest of piece, placing sts as for chart I. Work even until piece measures 5½ (6½, 7, 8)"/14 (16.5, 17.5, 20.5)cm from beg, end with a WS row.

**Divide for fronts and back**

**Next row (RS)** Place first and last 27 (29, 32, 35) sts on holders for fronts. Work on center 59 (65, 71, 75) sts in pat as established for back until piece measures 10 (11, 12, 13)"/25.5 (28, 30.5, 33)cm from beg. Bind off.

### RIGHT FRONT

With RS facing, cont in pat on 27 (29, 32, 35) sts from right holder until piece measures 6 (7, 8, 9)"/15.5 (17.5, 20.5, 23)cm from beg, end with a WS row.

**Neck shaping**

**Next row (RS)** Dec 1 st (neck edge), work to end. Cont to dec 1 st at neck edge every other row 2 (2, 4, 8) times more, then every 4th row 4 (4, 3, 1) times—20 (22, 24, 25) sts. Work even until same length as back. Bind off.

### LEFT FRONT

Work to correspond to right front, reversing neck shaping.

### RIGHT SLEEVE

With smaller needles and F [E], cast on 30 (30, 34, 34) sts. P 1 row, k 1 row.

**Beg rib pat**

**Row 1 (RS)** K2 D [A], *k2 A [D], k2 D [A]; rep from * to end.

**Row 2** P2 D [A], *k2 A [D], p2 D [A]; rep from * to end.

**Row 3** K2 D [A], *p2 A [D], k2 D [A]; rep from * to end.

Rep rows 2 and 3 twice more. With E [C], p 2 rows, k 1 row, inc 4 (6, 4, 4) sts evenly on last row—34 (36, 38, 38) sts. Change to larger needles and work in St st as foll:

**Beg chart III**

**Row 1 (RS)** Using appropriate chart for selected version, work sts 2-8 (1-8, 8, 8), work sts 1-8 to last 3 (4, 5, 5) sts, then work sts 1-3 (1-4, 1-5, 1-5). Rep rows 1-8 of chart III for rem of right sleeve, AT SAME TIME, inc 1 st each side (working inc sts into pat) every other row 5 (2, 4, 0) times, then every 4th row 3 (5, 5, 9) times—50 (50, 56, 56) sts. Work even until piece measures 6½ (7, 7½, 11)"/16.5 (17.5, 19, 28)cm from beg. Bind off.

### LEFT SLEEVE

With smaller needles and F [C], cast on 30 (30, 34, 34) sts. P 1 row, k 1 row.

**Beg rib pat**

**Row 1 (RS)** K2 B [F], *k2 C [E], k2 B [F]; rep from * to end.

**Row 2** P2 B [F], *k2 C [E], p2 B [F]; rep from * to end.

**Row 3** K2 B [F], *p2 C [E], k2 B [F]; rep from * to end.

Work as for right sleeve to beg of chart. Complete to correspond to right sleeve, working chart IV instead of chart III.

### FINISHING

Sew shoulder seams.

**Band**

With RS facing, circular needle and D [C], beg at lower right front edge, pick up and k 126 (138, 150, 162) sts evenly along right front, back neck and left front.

**Row 1 (WS)** Knit.
**Row 2** Purl.
**Row 3** P2 B [A], *p2 C [D], p2 B [A]; rep from * to end.
**Row 4** K2 B [A], *p2 C [D], k2 B [A]; rep from * to end.
Place marker for 4 buttonholes evenly spaced between beg of neck shaping and lower edge, on right side for girl's, and on left side for boy's.
**Row 5** [Work to marker, bind off 2 sts] 4 times, work to end.
**Row 6** Rep row 4, casting on 2 sts over bound-off sts.
**Rows 7 and 9** Rep row 5 omitting buttonholes.
**Row 8** Rep row 4.
**Row 10 (RS)** With F [E], knit, picking up 1 st in left front corner, pick up 1 st in each st at lower edge of body, pick up 1 st in right front corner; do not turn at end of row—238 (262, 282, 306) sts.
**Rnd 11 (RS)** Purl around. Bind off all sts purlwise.
Sew buttons opposite buttonholes.
With tapestry needle, work duplicate stitch on charts I and II with accent color.
Set in sleeves. Sew sleeve seams.

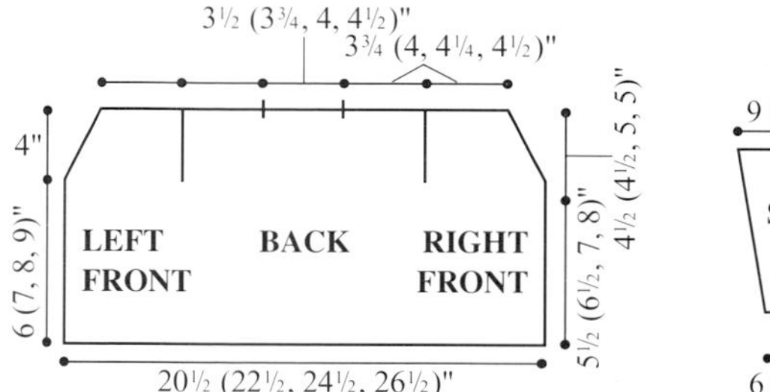


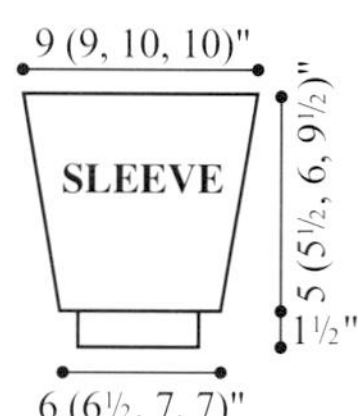

**DUPLICATE STITCH**

*Duplicate stitch covers a knit stitch. Bring the needle up below the stitch to be worked. Insert the needle under both loops one row above and pull it through. Insert it back into the stitch below and through the center of the next stitch in one motion, as shown.*

**Color key - Floral Border Version**

Turquoise (A)

Red (B)

Mustard (C)

Coral (D)

Teal (E)

Green (F)

**CHART I**
**Floral Border Version**

12
10
1
10 1

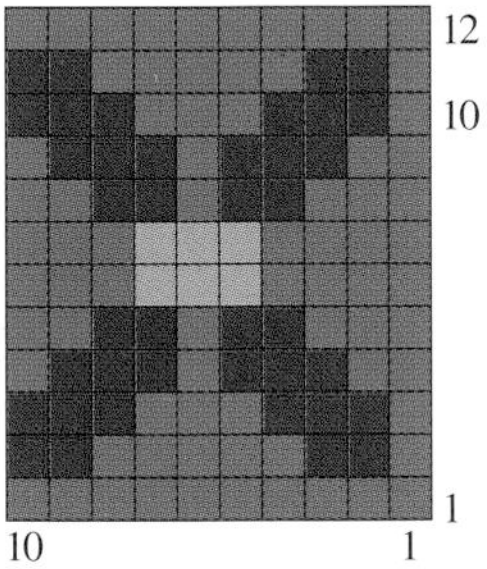

**CHART II**
**Floral Border Version**

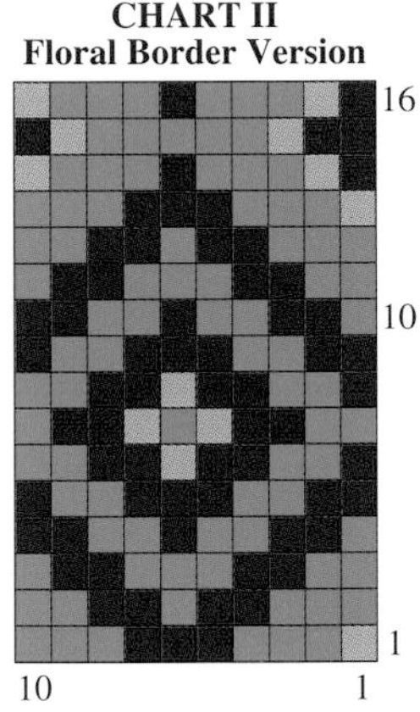


**CHART III**
**Floral Border Version**

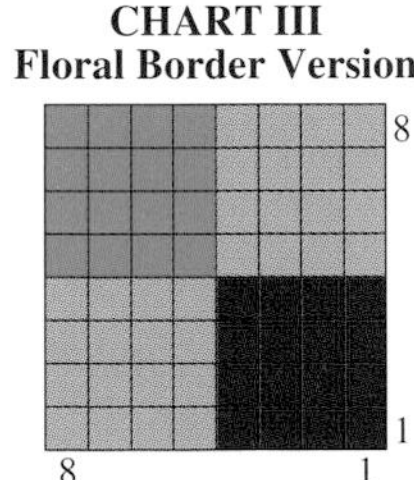


**CHART IV**
**Floral Border Version**

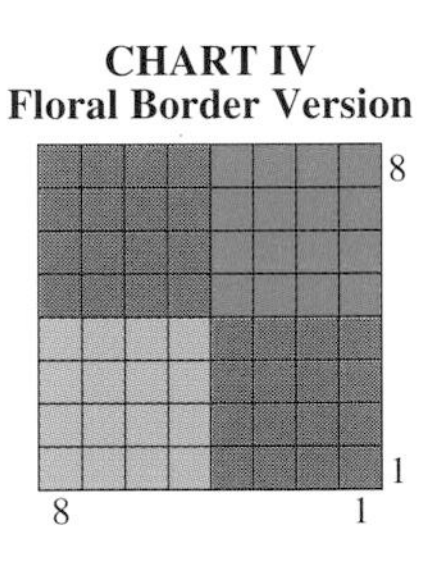

**Color key - Square Border Version**

- Turquoise (A)
- Daffodil (B)
- Navy (C)
- Coral (D)
- Green (E)
- Pink (F)

**CHART I**
**Square Border Version**

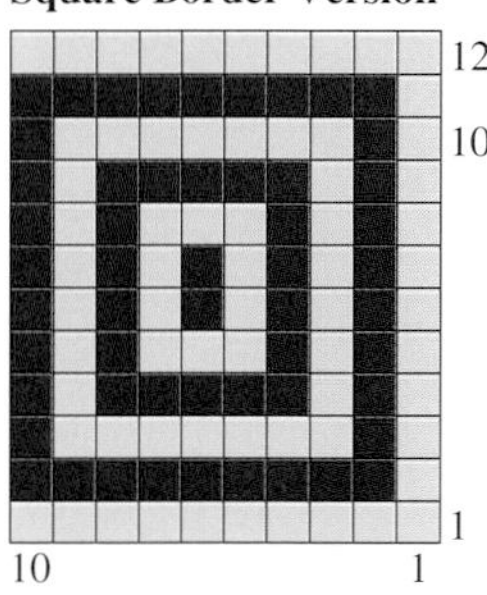


**CHART II**
**Square Border Version**

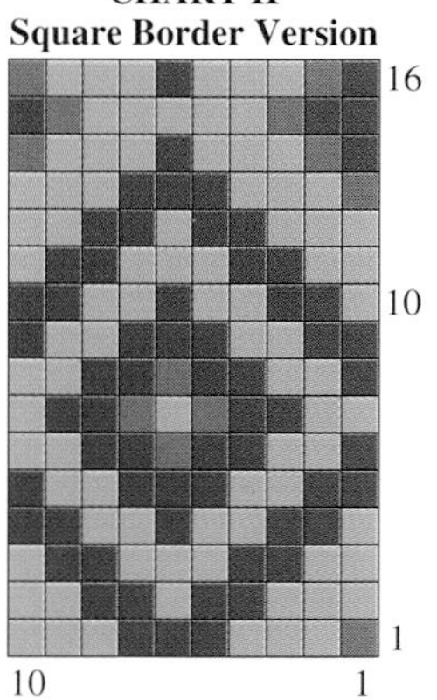


**CHART III**
**Square Border Version**

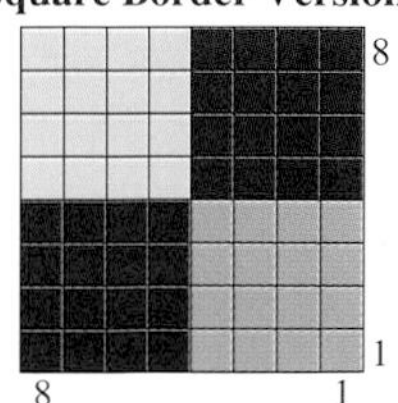


**CHART VI**
**Square Border Version**

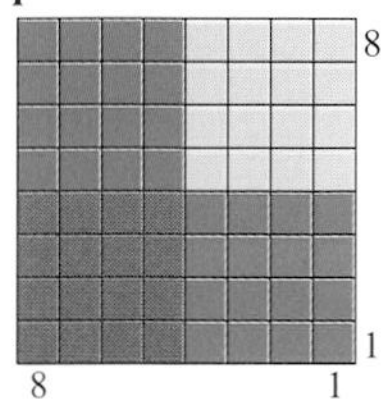

# TWO-PIECE SET

*Classic revival in baby brights*

*For Experienced Knitters*

**Surplice wrap top features a pattern of seed-stitch within a basketweave. The top is knit in one piece with T-square construction and faux raglan sleeves. The little knee pants, knit in seed-stitch, feature buttoning suspenders. Designed by Mari Lynn Patrick.**

### SIZES

Instructions are written for size 6-12 months.

### KNITTED MEASUREMENTS

**Jacket**

- Chest 23"/58.5cm
- Length 9½"/24cm
- Upper arm 8½"/21.5cm

**Pants**

- Hip 24½"/62cm
- Length 8½"/21.5cm

### MATERIALS

- 5 1¾/50g balls (each approx 248yd/225m) of Schaffhauser/Skacel *Mon Amour* (wool①) in #82 yellow
- Sizes 1 and 2 (2.5 and 2.75mm) knitting needles *or size to obtain gauge*
- Size 1 (2mm) steel crochet hook
- Stitch markers
- Three small novelty buttons

### GAUGE

30 sts and 54 rows to 4"/10cm over seed st OR basketweave pat using larger needles. *Take time to check gauge.*

### STITCH GLOSSARY

**Basketweave Pattern**

(multiple of 14 sts plus 2)

**Row 1 (RS)** Knit.

**Rows 2, 4 and 6** P2, *[k1, p1] twice, k1, p2; rep from *, to end.

**Rows 3, 5, and 7** K3, *p1, k1, p1, k4; rep from *, end last rep k3 instead of k4.

**Row 8** P2, *k12, p2; rep from * to end.

**Row 9** K2, *p12, k2; rep from * to end.

**Row 10** Purl.

**Rows 11, 13 and 15** K2, *[p1, k1] twice, p1, k2; rep from * to end.

**Rows 12, 14 and 16** P3, *k1, p1, k1, p4; rep from *, end last rep p3 instead of p4.

**Row !7** P7, *k2, p12; rep from *, end k2, p7.

**Row 18** K7, *p2, k12; rep from *, end p2, k7.

Rep rows 1-18 for basketweave pat.

**Seed Stitch**

**Row 1** *K1, p1; rep from *, end k1.

**Row 2** K the purl and p the knit sts. Rep row 2 for seed st.

### JACKET

### BACK

With smaller needles, cast on 82 sts. P 1 row. K 1 row. P 1 row. K 1 row, inc 6 sts evenly spaced across—88 sts. Change to larger needles. Working a k1 selvage st at beg and end of row, work in basketweave pat until piece measures approx 5"/12.5cm from beg, ending with pat row 10 of 4th rep.

**Beg sleeves**

**Note** Read before beg to knit. While casting on sts each side to add outwards for sleeves, sts are displaced from basketweave to seed st to create a slanting "faux" raglan. Displace sts for raglan as foll:

**Row 1 (RS)** Cast on 13 sts at beg of row and work these cast on sts in seed st, M1 in seed st, place marker (for back), p1, k1, ssk, work pat to within 4 sts of end of row, k2tog, k1, p1.

**Row 2 (WS)** Cast on 13 sts at beg of row and work these cast-on sts in seed st, M1 in seed st, place marker (for back), k1, p2, work pat st to 3 sts before marker, p2, k1, work seed st to end.

**Row 3 (Raglan slant row)** Cast on 4 sts and * work to first marker in seed st, M1 in seed st, sl marker, p1, k1, ssk, work pat to within 4 sts of second marker, k2tog, k1, p1, sl marker, M1 in seed st, work seed st to end*.

**Row 4** Cast on 4 sts and work to first marker in seed st, k1, p2, work to 3 sts before 2nd marker, p2, k1, work seed st to end. Cont to add on sts for sleeves by casting on 4 sts at beg of next 12 rows, 10 sts at beg of next 2 rows for a total of 190 sts, and AT SAME TIME, work raglan slant row 3 (by rep between *'s) every other row 12 times more, then work raglan slant row 3 every alternate 4th and 2nd row a total of 10 times. Work even so that you end with pat row 17 of 7th rep. There are 40 sts between markers for back neck and 75 sts each side in seed st for sleeves. Back is completed.

**Beg fronts**

**Next row (WS)** Place marker at beg of row (to mark ½ sleeve), work until there are 77 sts on needle, bind off center 36 sts for back neck, join another ball of yarn and work to end, place marker at end of row (to mark ½ sleeve). Cont to work both sides at once with separate balls of yarn.

**Next row (RS)** Work 75 sts in seed st, p1, k1 (selvage st) for right front and sleeve; then for left front and sleeve, k1 (selvage st), p1, work 75 sts in seed st. Work even for 9 more rows on the 77 sts each side.

**Next row (RS)** Work 74 sts in seed st, p2tog, place marker, k1 into front, back and front of last st (for inc 2); inc 2 sts in first st, place marker, p2tog, work 74 sts in seed st.

**Next row** Work seed st to last 5 sts, p1, k1, p2, k1; k1, p2, k1, p1, seed st to end.

**Next row** Work to 2 sts before marker, p2tog, k2, place 2nd marker, M1, inc 1 in last st; work other side to correspond. Beg with 3rd row of basketweave, cont to inc 1 st at each neck edge every other row (working incs into basketweave) and AT SAME TIME, displace sts by p2tog before first marker and M1 after 2nd marker 15 times more. There are 94 sts. Then cont to displace sts and inc as before 8 times more, bind off from sleeve edge 10 sts once, 4 sts 7 times and 13 sts once. Then cont in front sts only, leaving side seam straight, cont to inc 1 st at front edge only every other row 7 times more—58 sts. Work even until there are same number of pat blocks to match back up to hem. P next row on WS dec 3 sts evenly spaced—55 sts. Change to smaller needles. [P 1 row, k 1 row] twice. Bind off purlwise. Finish left front and sleeve in same way.

### FINISHING

Block jacket to measurements. With smaller needles, pick up and k 30 sts along center front, place marker, 46 sts along shaped neck, 6 sts along top of sleeve, 34 sts along back neck and other side to correspond. Inc 1 st each side of corner markers every WS row 3 times, p 1 row, [p 1 row, k 1 row] twice. Bind off purlwise. Pick up and k 47 sts along sleeve cuff edge and work rolled edge in same way.

### TIE

With larger needles, cast on 150 sts. Work in seed st for 9 rows. Bind off in pat. With crochet hook, work edge all around tie as foll: Join at one long edge and working backwards (left to right), * work 1 backwards sc into st 2 rows below edge, ch 2, skip ½"/1.25 cm; rep from * to short end, ch 8 for buttonloop, cont sc edge around. Sew tie to right front 3¼"/8.5cm from lower edge. Sew right side seam and sleeve seams. Sew left side seam leaving a 1"/2.5cm opening 3¼"/8.5cm from lower edge for tie. Sew button opposite buttonloop.

### PANTS

### BACK

With smaller needles, cast on 42 sts for left leg.

**Row 1 (RS)** K1 (selvage st), *k2, k1, p1; rep from * to last st, k1 (selvage st).

**Row 2** K1,*p1, k1, p2; rep from *, end k1.

Rep these 2 rows for rib for a total of 12 rows or 1"/2.5cm from beg. P 1 row on RS. Change to larger needles and cont in seed st for 1"/2.5cm more. Cast on 8 sts at end of row and leave sts on a holder. Work right leg to correspond (but do not cast on at end of last row). On next RS row, work 42 sts of right leg, 50 sts of left leg—92 sts. Cont in seed st until piece measures 7¼"/18.5cm from beg of leg. K next WS row dec 6 sts evenly spaced—86 sts. Change to smaller needles and work in rib as on lower edge for 1¼"/3cm. Bind off in rib. Work front same as back, only working two 3-st buttonholes when waistband measures ¾"/1.25cm as foll: Work 27 sts, bind off 3 sts, work 26 sts, bind off 3 sts, work to end.

### FINISHING

Block pieces to measurements. Sew side and inside leg seams. For straps, with larger needles, cast on 98 sts. Work in seed st for 8 rows. Bind off in pat. Work crochet edge around straps as on jacket band. Sew buttons to ends of straps. Sew straps to center back, securing in place for 1"/2.5cm from top edge.

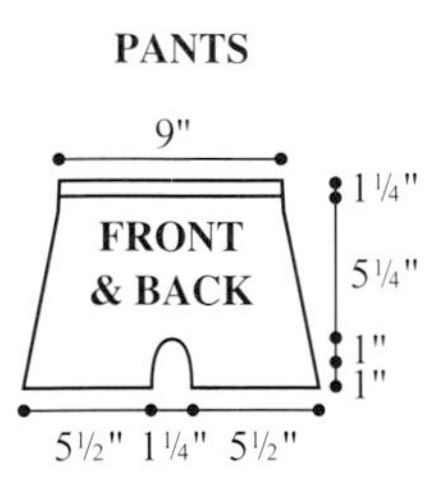


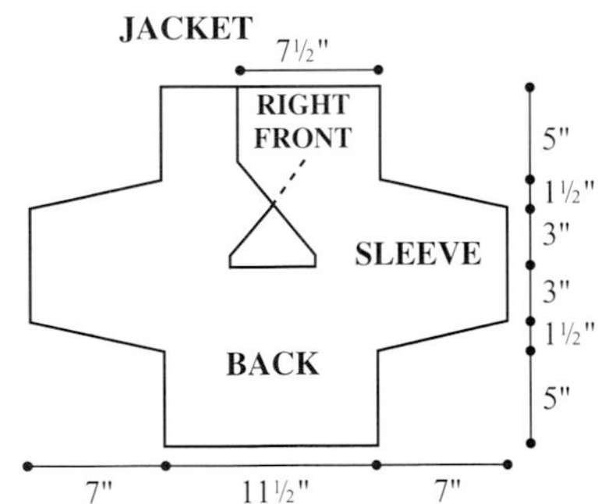

# PANDA

*Beary special*

*For Intermediate Knitters*

**Cuddly panda bear keeps warm in his own ribbed scarf. He's knit in soft bouclé yarn, and has button-jointed arms and legs. Designed by the Cleckheaton Design Studio.**

**KNITTED MEASUREMENTS**

- 20"/52cm tall

**MATERIALS**

- 3 1¾oz/50g skeins (each approx 104yd/95m) of Cleckheaton *Wool Bouclé* by Plymouth(wool⑤) each in #1890 cream (MC) and #1896 black (A).
- 1 1¾oz/50g skeins (each approx 105yd/96m) of Cleckheaton *Country 8-ply* by Plymouth (wool③) in #1872 red (B)
- One pair each sizes 6 and 7 (4 and 4.5mm) needles *or size to obtain gauge*
- Stitch markers and holders
- Small amount of smooth yarn for sewing
- Four 1"/25mm black buttons
- 1yd/1m narrow black elastic
- Safety eyes and nose
- Fiberfill

**GAUGE**

16 sts and 25 rows to 4"/10cm over St st using larger needles and *Wool Bouclé*. *Take time to check gauge.*

**BACK**

With larger needles and MC, cast on 4 sts.

**Row 1** Knit, inc 1 in each st across—8 sts.

**Row 2** P3, [inc in next st] twice, p3.

**Row 3** Inc in first st, k3, [inc in next st] twice, k3, inc in last st.

**Row 4** P6, [inc in next st] twice, p6.

**Row 5** K7, [inc in next st] twice, k7.

**Row 6** P8, [inc in next st] twice, p8.

**Row 7** Inc in first st, k8, [inc in next st] twice, k8, inc in last st—24 sts.

**Row 8 and all WS rows** Purl.

**Row 9** K11, [inc in next st] twice, k11.

**Row 11** Inc in first st, k11, [inc in next st] twice, k11, inc in last st.

**Row 13** K14, [inc in next st] twice, k14.

**Row 15** Inc in first st, k14, [inc in next st] twice, k14, inc in last st.

**Row 17** K17, [inc in next st] twice, k17.

**Row 19** Inc in first st, k17, [inc in next st] twice, k17, inc in last st—42 sts. Work in St st for 3 rows.

**Next row (RS)** Inc in first st, k19, [inc in next st] twice, k19, inc in last st. Cont in St st, inc 1 st each side every 4th row twice—50 sts. Work even in St st for 6 rows. Cont in St st, dec 1 st each side every 4th row 4 times—42 sts.

**Next row** P19, [p2tog] twice, p19.

**Next row** K18, [k2tog] twice, k18.

**Next row** P17, [p2tog] twice, p17.

**Next row** K2tog, k14, [k2tog] twice, k14, k2tog.

**Next row** P14, [p2tog] twice, p14.

**Next row** K13, [k2tog] twice, k13.

**Next row** P12, [p2tog] twice, p12.

**Next row** K2tog, k9, [k2tog] twice, k9, k2tog.

**Next row** P2tog, p7, [k2tog] twice, p7, p2tog. Bind off rem 18 sts.

**FRONT**

With larger needles and MC, cast on 4 sts.

**Row 1** Knit.

**Row 2 and all WS rows** Purl.

**Row 3** Knit, inc 1 in each st across—8 sts.

**Row 5** K3, [inc in next st] twice, k3.

**Row 7** Inc in first st, k3, [inc in next st] twice, k3, inc in last st.

**Row 9** K6, [inc in next st] twice, k6.

**Row 11** Inc in first st, k6, [inc in next st]

twice, k6, inc in last st. Cont in this way to inc 2 sts then 4 sts alternately every other row until there are 50 sts. Work 3 rows even. Inc 1 st each side of next row—52 sts. Work 7 rows even.

**Next row** K2tog, k22, [k2tog] twice, k22, k2tog. Work 3 rows even.

**Next row** K2tog, k20, [k2tog] twice, k20, k2tog. Work 3 rows even.

**Next row** K2tog, k18, [k2tog] twice, k18, k2tog. Work 3 rows even.

**Next row** K2tog, k16, [k2tog] twice, k16, k2tog. Work 1 row even.

**Next row** K16, [k2tog] twice, k16. Work 1 row even.

**Next row** K2tog, k13, [k2tog] twice, k13, k2tog. Work 1 row even.

**Next row** K13, [k2tog] twice, k13. Work 1 row even.

**Next row** K2tog, k10, [k2tog] twice, k10, k2tog.

**Next row** P2tog, p8, [k2tog] twice, p8, p2tog. Bind off rem 20 sts.

## HEAD

### Right side

With larger needles and MC, cast on 18 sts. Beg with a knit row, work in St st for 2 rows.

**Row 3** K, inc 1 st each side.

**Rows 4 and 6** Purl.

**Row 5** K, inc 1 st in last st.

**Row 7** Inc 1 in first st, k to end.

**Row 8** Cast on 2 sts, p to end—24 sts.

**Row 9** Knit.

**Row 10** Rep row 8. Rep last 4 rows twice—36 sts.

**Next row** Rep row 7. Work 2 rows even. Bind off 2 sts at beg of next row—35 sts. Dec 1 st at end of next row, then cont to dec 1 st at same edge every other row 3 times more—31 sts. Work 1 row even. Dec 1 st each side of next side then every other row until 9 sts rem. Bind off.

### Left side

Work as for right side, reversing shaping.

## GUSSET

With larger needles and MC, cast on 7 sts. Work in St st for 4 rows, inc 1 st each side of next row, then inc 1 each side every 6th row until there are 21 sts. Work 5 rows even. Dec 1 st each side of next row, then every 4th row 6 times, every other row twice—3 sts. Work 1 row even.

**Next row** K1, k2tog.

**Next row** P2tog, fasten off.

## EYE PATCHES

With larger needles and A, cast on 4 sts.

**Rows 1 and 3** Knit.

**Row 2** P4, inc in last st.

**Row 4** P, inc 1 st each side.

Work 2 rows even.

**Row 7** K, inc 1 st each side—9 sts.

Work 2 rows even.

**Row 10** P2tog, p to end.

**Row 11** K2tog, k to end. P 1 row.

**Row 13** K2tog, k to end.

**Row 14** P2tog, p to end. Bind off rem 5 sts.

## EARS

With larger needles and A, cast on 18 sts. Work in St st for 8 rows. Dec 1 st each side every other row 3 times, *every* row 3 times—6 sts. Work 2 rows even. Inc 1 st each side *every* row 3 times, every other row 3 times—18 sts. Work 7 rows even. Bind off.

## ARMS

### Left half (make 2)

With larger needles and A, cast on 2 sts. K 1 row, inc 1 st each side.

**Next row** Inc in first st, p to end.

**Next row** K, inc 1 st each side. Rep last 2 rows twice—13 sts. Cont in St st, inc 1 st at end of every WS row 3 times. Work 1 row even.

**Next row** K2tog, k to last st, inc in last st.

**Next row** Purl. Rep last 2 rows 4 times more—16 sts. Work 6 rows even. Inc 1 st at beg of next and foll 4th row—18 sts. Work 3 rows even.

**Next row** Inc in first st, k to last 2 sts, k2tog. Rep last 4 rows 5 times more—18 sts. Work 1 row even. Cont in St st, dec 1 st each side every row 6 times. Bind off rem 6 sts.

**Right half** (make 2)

Work as for left half, reversing shaping.

### LEGS

**Left half** (make 2)

With larger needles and A, cast on 26 sts. Work in St st for 2 rows. Dec 1 st at end of next row, then cont to dec 1 st at same edge *every* row 4 times more, then every other row twice, every 4th row twice—17 sts. Work 5 rows even. Inc 1 st each side of next row—19 sts. Work 6 rows even.

**Next row** Inc 1 st each side. Work 7 rows even. Rep last inc row—23 sts. Work 5 rows even. Dec 1 st each side next row, then every 4th row once, every other row twice, *every* row 5 times. Bind off rem 5 sts.

**Right half** (make 2)

Work as for left half, reversing shaping.

**Sole** (make 2)

With larger needles and A, cast on 4 sts. Work in St st for 2 rows. Cast on 2 sts at beg of next 2 rows, inc 1 st each side every row twice—12 sts. Work 14 rows even. Dec 1 st each side every other row twice, *every* row 3 times.

**Next row** K2tog, fasten off.

### FINISHING

Use smooth yarn for sewing. Sew pairs of leg tog, stuff, sew sole to bottom of foot. Foll diagram, join left and right head pieces tog from neck to tip of nose. Sew head gusset between head pieces so that gusset ends at tip of nose, leave neck edge open. Foll manufacturer's directions, attach nose. Sew on eye patches. Attach eyes in center of patches. Join front and back body pieces, leaving neck edge open. Sew pairs of arms tog, leaving an opening for stuffing. Firmly stuff body, head and arms. Sew arm openings closed. Sew head to body, adding additional stuffing if necessary to make neck firm. Fold ears in half and sew side seams, then sew to head. Attach arms and legs by stitching through button, then through arm or leg, bear body, rem arm or leg, then 2nd button with elastic.

**Scarf**

With smaller needles and B, cast on 18 sts.

**Row 1** K3, *p2, k3; rep from * to end.

**Row 2** P3, *k2, p3; rep from * to end.

Rep these 2 rows until piece measures 31"/78cm, end with row 2. Bind off loosely in rib. With B, make 8 small tassels. Sew 4 to each end of scarf. Tie scarf around panda's neck.

HOW TO ASSEMBLE TEDDY

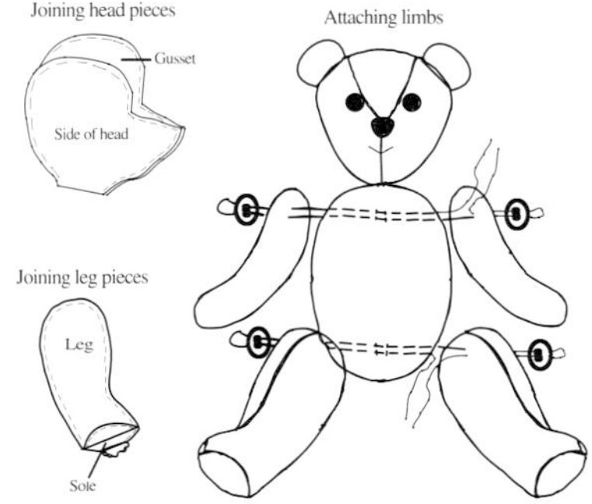

# RIBBED WAISTCOAT

*Vested interest*

**Marled yarn lends a casual air to this easy vest. Knit in the round to the armholes, it features buttoned shoulders and rolled edges. Designed by Victoria Mayo.**

**SIZES**

Instructions are written for size 6 months. Changes for sizes 12 and 18-24 months are in parentheses.

**KNITTED MEASUREMENTS**

- Chest 21½ (24, 26½)"/54.5 (61, 67.5)cm
- Length 10 (10½, 13)"/25.5 (26.5, 33)cm

**MATERIALS**

- 1 (1, 2) 3½oz/100g balls (each approx 200yd/182m) of Spinrite *Muskosa* (wool④) in #9836 denim marl
- Size 6 (4mm) circular needle, 24"/60cm long *or size to obtain gauge*
- Three ½"/15mm buttons
- Stitch holders

**GAUGE**

21 sts and 28 rows to 4"/10cm over k5, p2 rib (blocked) using size 6 (4mm) needle. *Take time to check gauge.*

**Note** Body is worked in one piece to the underarm.

**STITCH GLOSSARY**

**K5, P2 Rib**

(multiple of 7 sts)

**In the round**

**Rnd 1 (RS)** *P1, k5, p1; rep from * around.

Rep rnd 1 for k5, p2 rib.

**Straight**

**Row 1 (RS)** *P1, k5, p1; rep from * to end.

**Row 2** K the knit sts and p the purl sts.

Rep row 2 for k5, p2 rib.

**BODY**

Cast on 112 (126, 140) sts. Join, taking care not to twist sts on needle. Mark end of rnd and sl marker every rnd. Work in rnds of k1, p1 rib for 1"/2.5cm. Cont to work in rnds of k5, p2 rib until piece measures 5½ (5½, 7½)"/14 (14, 19)cm.

**Divide for back and front**

**Next row** Bind off 2 (3, 3) sts for armhole, work until there are 54 (60, 67) sts on RH needle for back, place rem sts on a holder for front. Cont to work back and forth on back sts only as foll: Bind off 2 (3, 3) sts at beg of next row, then bind off 2 sts at beg of next 2 rows, 1 st at beg of next 4 rows—44 (49, 56) sts. Work even until armhole measures 4½ (5, 5½)"/11.5 (12.5, 14)cm, end with a WS row.

**Next row (RS)** Bind off 32 (35, 39) sts, work rem 12 (14, 17) sts of left shoulder in k1, p1 rib for 1"/2.5cm for button flap. Bind off in rib.

**FRONT**

Work sts from front holder, and work armhole shaping as for back. Work even until armhole measures 1½ (2, 2)"/4 (5, 5)cm, end with a WS row.

**Neck shaping**

**Next row (RS)** Work 22 (24, 28) sts, join 2nd ball of yarn and bind off center 0 (1, 0) st, work to end. Working both sides at once, dec 1 st at each neck edge every other row 10 (10, 11) times, AT SAME TIME, when armhole measures 3½ (4, 4½)"/9 (10, 1.5)cm, work 12 (14, 17) sts of left shoulder in k1, p1 rib for ½"/1.5cm, end with a WS row.

**Next row (RS)** Rib 1 st, [yo, k2tog, rib 2 (3, 4)] twice, yo, k2tog, work to end. Complete as for back.

## FINISHING

Block pieces to measurements.

### Neckband

With RS facing, pick up and k 66 (70, 78) sts evenly around neck. Beg with a p row, work in St st for 5 rows. Bind off knitwise on RS.

### Armhole band

With RS facing, pick up and k 58 (66, 72) sts evenly around each armhole edge. Work as for neckband. Sew right shoulder and armhole band seam. Sew left armhole band seam only. Sew buttons to back flap opposite buttonholes.

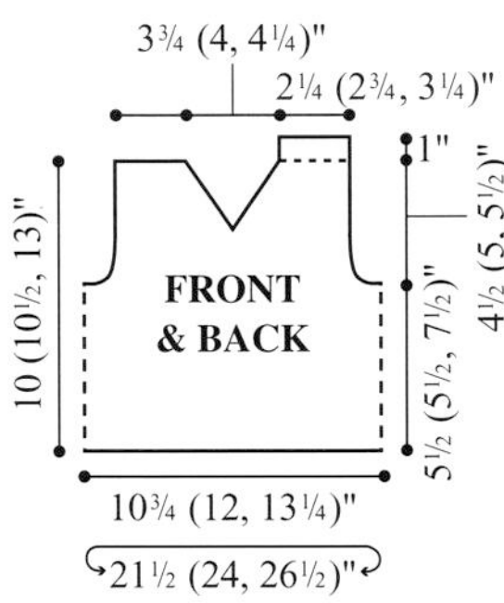

# CHENILLE COAT

*Mode in miniature*

**Cozy chenille for the urban baby. Easy coat combines empire styling with a full skirt that decreases to a buttoned bodice. Designed by Lila P. Chin.**

### SIZES

Instructions are written for size 12 months. Changes for sizes 18 and 24 months are in parentheses.

### KNITTED MEASUREMENTS

- Chest (buttoned) 23 (24, 25)"/58.5 (61, 63.5)cm
- Length 15 (16, 18)"/38 (40.5, 46)cm
- Upper arm 11 (12, 13)"/28 (30.5, 33)cm

### MATERIALS

- 5 (6, 7) 1¾oz/50g balls (each approx 99yds/90m) of Ad Hoc/Filatura Di Crosa *Antares* (polyamid/wool⑤) in #402 pink
- Size 4 (3.5mm) circular needle, 24"/60cm long *or size to obtain gauge*
- Four ½"/13mm buttons
- Stitch holders and markers

### GAUGE

20 sts and 32 rows to 4"/10cm over St st using size 4 (3.5mm) needles.
*Take time to check gauge.*

**Note** Body of sweater is worked in one piece to the underarm.

### BODY

Cast on 170 (180, 190) sts and work in garter st for 1"/2.5cm.

**Next row** K5, pm, k 160 (170, 180), pm, k5.

**Next row** K5, sl marker, p 160 (170, 180), sl marker, k5.

Cont in St st as established, keeping the first and last 5 sts in garter st for bands, until piece measures 9 (9½, 11)"/23 (24, 28)cm from beg, end with a WS row.

**Next row (RS)** K, dec 50 (54, 60) sts evenly spaced—120 (126, 130) sts. Cont in garter st over all sts for 7 rows more.

**Divide for fronts and back**

**Next row (RS)** K3, k2tog, yo (buttonhole), work until there are 31 (33, 34) sts on RH needle and place on a holder for right front, bind off 5 sts, work until there are 53 (55, 57) sts on RH needle for back, place rem 31 (33, 34) sts on holder for left front. Cont to work on back sts only in St st as foll: bind off 5 sts at beg of next row, then dec 1 st each side every other row 3 times—42 (44, 46) sts. Work even until armhole measures 5 (5½, 6)"/12.5 (14, 15.5)cm. Bind off.

### RIGHT FRONT

**Next row (WS)** Place sts from right front holder to needle to work next row on WS and bind off 5 sts (armhole edge), work to end. Dec 1 st at armhole edge every other row 3 times—23 (25, 26) sts. Work even, working 2 more buttonholes 1"/2.5cm apart, until armhole measures 3 (3½, 4)"/7.5 (9, 10.5)cm, end with a WS row.

**Neck shaping**

**Next row (RS)** Bind off 5 (6, 6) sts (neck edge), work to end. Cont to bind off from neck edge 3 sts once, 2 sts twice, dec 1 st every other row 1 (2, 2) times. Work even until same length as back. Bind off rem 10 (10, 11) sts for shoulder.

### LEFT FRONT

Work to correspond to right front, reversing shaping and omitting buttonholes.

## SLEEVES

Cast on 30 (32, 34) sts and work in garter st for 1"/2.5cm. Cont in St st, inc 1 st each side every 2nd (2nd, 4th) row 13 (14, 15) times—56 (60, 64) sts. Work until piece measures 5½ (6½, 9½)"/14 (16.5, 24)cm from beg.

### Cap shaping

Dec 5 (6, 6) sts at beg of next 2 rows, 3 sts at beg of next 2 rows. Dec 1 st each side every other row 8 (8, 10) times, every 4th row 0 (1, 1) time. Bind off rem 24 sts.

## FINISHING

Lightly block pieces to measurements. Sew shoulder seams.

### Collar

With RS facing, pick up and k 36 (40, 44) sts evenly around neck edge. Work in garter st for 3"/7.5cm. Bind off loosely. Sew on buttons opposite buttonholes. Set in sleeves. Sew sleeve seams.

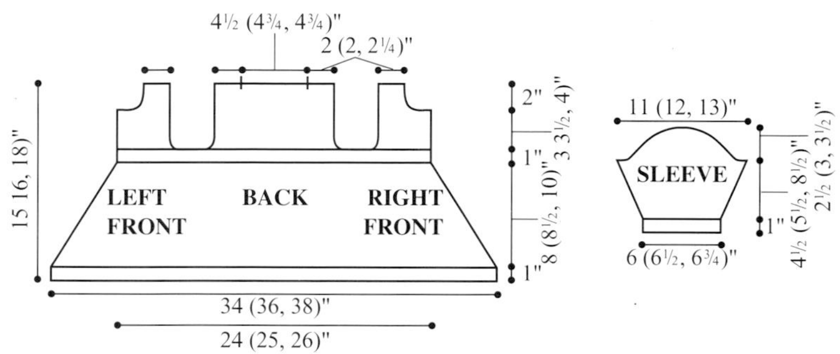


## WORKING WITH CHENILLE

*■ Don't be surprised by the needle size. Chenille takes a smaller needle than usually required for similar weight yarns. This creates a dense fabric and keeps the stitches in check, giving them less leeway to "worm" out of place into an uneven, loopy appearance.*

*■ Avoid over-twisting. Twisting crushes the pile and may cause stitches to curl out of place. The British method of knitting (throwing or casting yarn over the needle with the right hand) twists the yarn to a greater extent than the Continental, making the latter better suited to working with chenille. British-style knitters should guide the yarn over the needle without any extra twists.*

*■ Accustom yourself to yarn with very little "give." Work each stitch with a slight firmness to prevent any slack, but don't pull too tight—chenille may break when stretched.*

*■ Keep chenille free from fuzz and lint. Keep your working ball of yarn in a nylon spool protector, or resealable sandwich bag (use a twist tie if needed).*

# ROCKING-HORSE CARDIGAN

*Rock-a-bye baby*

*For Intermediate Knitters*

**Toys on parade edge this adorable rib-patterned cardigan. A charming old-fashioned rocking horse brightens up the back; perky patch pockets accent the front. Designed by Jean Moss.**

### SIZES

Instructions are written for size 6 months. Changes for sizes 12, 18 and 24 months are in parentheses.

### KNITTED MEASUREMENTS

- Chest (buttoned) 22½ (24½, 26¼, 27½)"/57 (62, 66.5, 69.5)cm
- Length 11½ (12, 13, 14)"/29.5 (31, 33, 35.5)cm
- Upper arm 11 (12, 12½, 13)"/28 (31, 32, 33)cm

### MATERIALS

- 3 (3, 4, 4) 1¾oz/50g hanks (each approx 176yd/162m) of Koigu Wool Designs *Premium Merino* (wool②) in #2151 aqua (A)
- 1 hank each #2393 cocoa (B), #2385 peach (C), #2340 olive (D), #2128 mauve (E), #2390 dk brown (F), #2392 coffee (G), #2323 blue (H), #0000 white (I), and #2239 purple (J)
- One pair each sizes 2 and 3 (2.5 and 3mm) needles *or size to obtain gauge*
- 2 stitch holders
- 1 stitch marker
- Tapestry needle
- Four ½"/25mm buttons

### GAUGE

28 sts and 43 rows to 4"/10cm over chart I (rows 17-22) using larger needles.
*Take time to check gauge.*

**Note** When changing colors, twist yarns on WS to prevent holes in work.

### STITCH GLOSSARY

**Double Moss Stitch**

**Row 1 (RS)** *P1, k2, p1; rep from * to end.
**Rows 2 and 4** K the knit sts and p the purl sts.
**Row 3** *K1, p2, k1; rep from * to end.
Rep rows 1-4 for double moss st.

### BACK

With smaller needles and A, cast on 77 (85, 89, 95) sts.Work in k1, p1 rib for 15 rows. K next row on WS for turning ridge.

**Beg chart I**

**Row 1 (RS)** Beg with st 34 (31, 29, 26) work to st 36, work sts 1-36 twice, then work sts 1-2 (7, 9, 12) once more. Cont in pat as established through row 16. Change to larger needles and A. Cont to rep rows 17-22 of chart I until piece measures 3¾ (4¼, 4½, 5)"/9.5 (10.5, 11.5, 12.5)cm above turning ridge, end with a WS row.

**Beg chart II**

**Row 1 (RS)** Work 19 (23, 25, 28) sts in pat, work 39 sts of chart II, work last 19 (23, 25, 28) sts in pat. Cont as established until piece measures measures 6 (6, 6¾, 7½)"/15.5 (15.5, 17, 19)cm above turning ridge, end with a WS row.

**Armhole shaping**

Bind off 6 (6, 7, 7) sts at beg of next 2 rows—65 (73, 75, 81) sts. Work even through row 57 of chart II. Cont all sts in chart I (rep rows 17-22 only) until armhole measures 5 (5½, 5¾, 6)"/12.5 (14, 14.5, 15)cm, end with a WS row.

**Neck shaping**

**Next row (RS)** Work 21 (24, 24, 26) sts, join 2nd ball of yarn and bind off center

23 (25, 27, 29) sts, work to end. Working both sides at once, dec 1 st at each neck edge every row 3 times. Work even until armhole measures 5½ (6, 6¼, 6½)"/14 (15.5, 16, 16.5)cm. Bind off rem 18 (21, 21, 23) sts each side for shoulders.

## LEFT FRONT

With smaller needles and A, cast on 39 (42, 45, 47) sts. Work as for back through turning ridge.

### Beg chart I

**Row 1 (RS)** Beg with st 34 (31, 28, 26) work to st 36, then work sts 1-36 once. Cont in pat as established through row 16. Change to larger needles and A. Cont to rep rows 17-22 of chart I until same length as back to armhole, end with a WS row.

### Armhole shaping

Bind off 6 (6, 7, 7) sts at beg of next row—33 (36, 38, 40) sts. Work even until armhole measures 1 (1, 1¼, 1½)"/2.5 (2.5, 3.5, 4)cm, end with a WS row.

### Neck shaping

Dec 1 st at end of next row (neck edge) and cont to dec 1 st at neck edge every other row 8 (5, 9, 9) times, every 4th row 6 (9, 7, 7) times—18 (21, 21, 23) sts. Work even until same length as back. Bind off.

### Left front pocket

With larger needles and J, cast on 18 sts. In St st, work rows 1-18 of chart III. Change to smaller needles and k next row with B. Work in double moss st for 4 rows. Bind off.

## RIGHT FRONT

Work as for left front, reversing all shaping and placement of chart I.

### Right front pocket

Work as for left front pocket, using G to cast on, and working chart IV instead of chart III.

## SLEEVES

With smaller needles and A, cast on 41 (43, 45, 47) sts. Work as for back through turning ridge.

### Beg chart I

**Row 1 (RS)** Beg with st 34 (34, 32, 31) work to st 36, work sts 1-36 once, then work sts 1-2 (4, 4, 5) of chart 1. Cont as established through row 16. Change to larger needles and A, and cont to rep rows 17-22 of chart I for rem of sleeve, AT SAME TIME, inc 1 st each side (working inc sts into pat) on next row, then every 2nd (2nd, 2nd, 6th) row 10 (14, 9, 9) times, every 4th row 7 (6, 11, 12) times—77 (85, 87, 91) sts. Work even until piece measures 7 (7¼, 8½, 12¼)"/17.5 (18.5, 21.5, 31)cm above turning ridge. Bind off.

## FINISHING

Sew shoulder seams.

### Collar and front bands

With RS facing, smaller needles and B, pick up and knit 48 (48, 54, 60) sts evenly along lower edge of left front at turning ridge to point where neck shaping beg, and leave on holder. Rep for right front edge. With RS facing, smaller needles and B, pick up and k 24 (26, 28, 30) sts across back of neck. P 1 row. Work in double moss st as foll:

**Row 1 (RS)** Work to end of row, pick up and k 1 st inside of first row on left front.

**Row 2** Cont in pat as established, work to end of row, pick up and p 1 st inside of first row on right front.

Cont as established picking up 1 st at end of next 44 (50, 56, 62) rows, then pick up 2 sts at end of next 12 (12, 14, 8) rows—94 (102, 102, 102) sts. You should now be at point where neck shaping begins.

**Front bands**

Cont in pat as established on collar and with RS facing, work across 48 (48, 54, 60) sts from right band holder, pm, work 94 (102, 102, 102) sts of collar and 48 (48, 54, 60) sts from left band holder—190 (198, 210, 222) sts. Place markers for 4 buttons on right front for girl's and left front for boy's, the first one ¼"/.5cm from lower edge, the last one just below neck shaping, and two others spaced evenly between.

**Next row** Work buttonholes on band opposite markers as foll: bind off 3 sts for each buttonhole. On next row, cast on 3 sts over bound-off sts. Work even for 1 row with B, then 1 row with C. Bind off in pat with C.

Set in sleeves, sewing last ¾ (¾, 1, 1)"/2 (2, 2.5, 25)cm at top of sleeve to bound-off armhole sts. Sew side and sleeve seams.

Fold all hems to WS at turning ridge and sew in place. Sew on buttons. Sew patch pockets ½ (½, ¾, ¾)"/1.5 (1.5, 2, 2)cm above chart I, centering on each front.

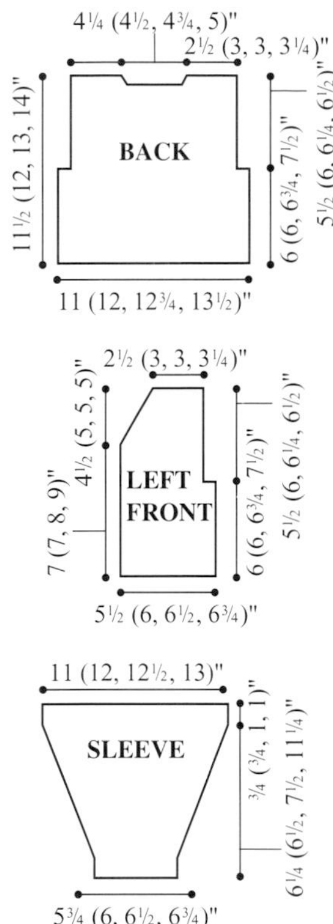

CHART I

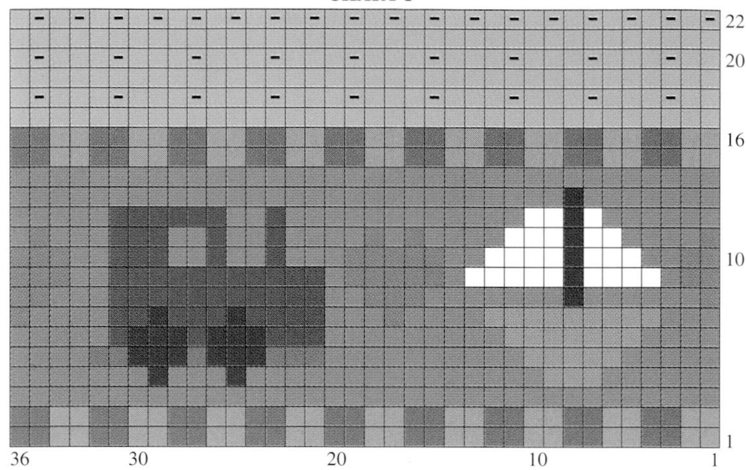
22
20
16
10
1
36
30
20
10
1

Color key
Aqua (A)
Aqua (A) P on RS rows, K on WS rows
Cocoa (B)
Peach (C)
Olive (D)
Mauve (E)
Dk Brown (F)
Coffee (G)
Blue (H)
White (I)
Purple (J)

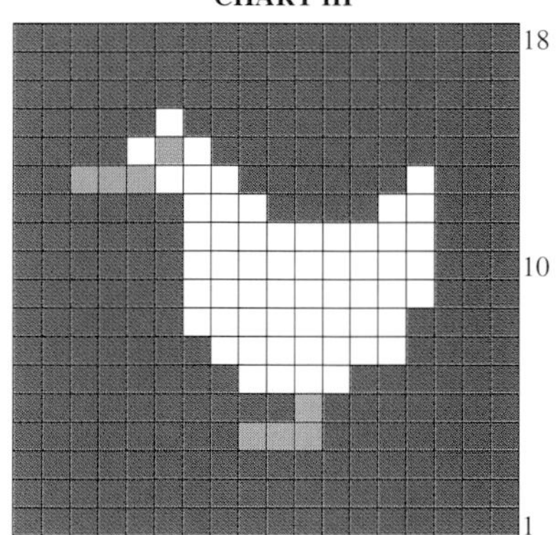
CHART III
18
10
1
18 sts

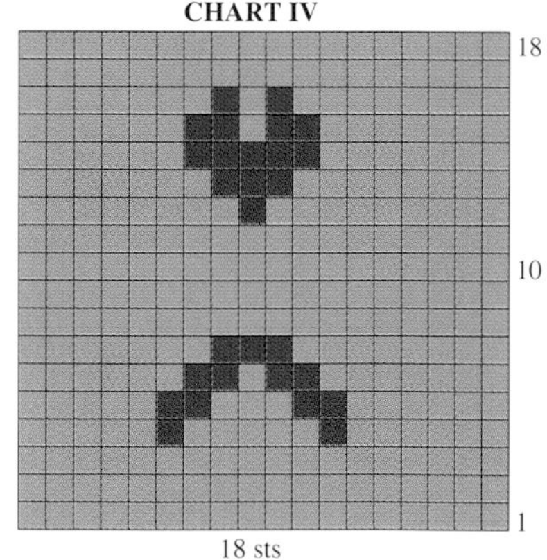
CHART IV
18
10
1
18 sts

## CHART II

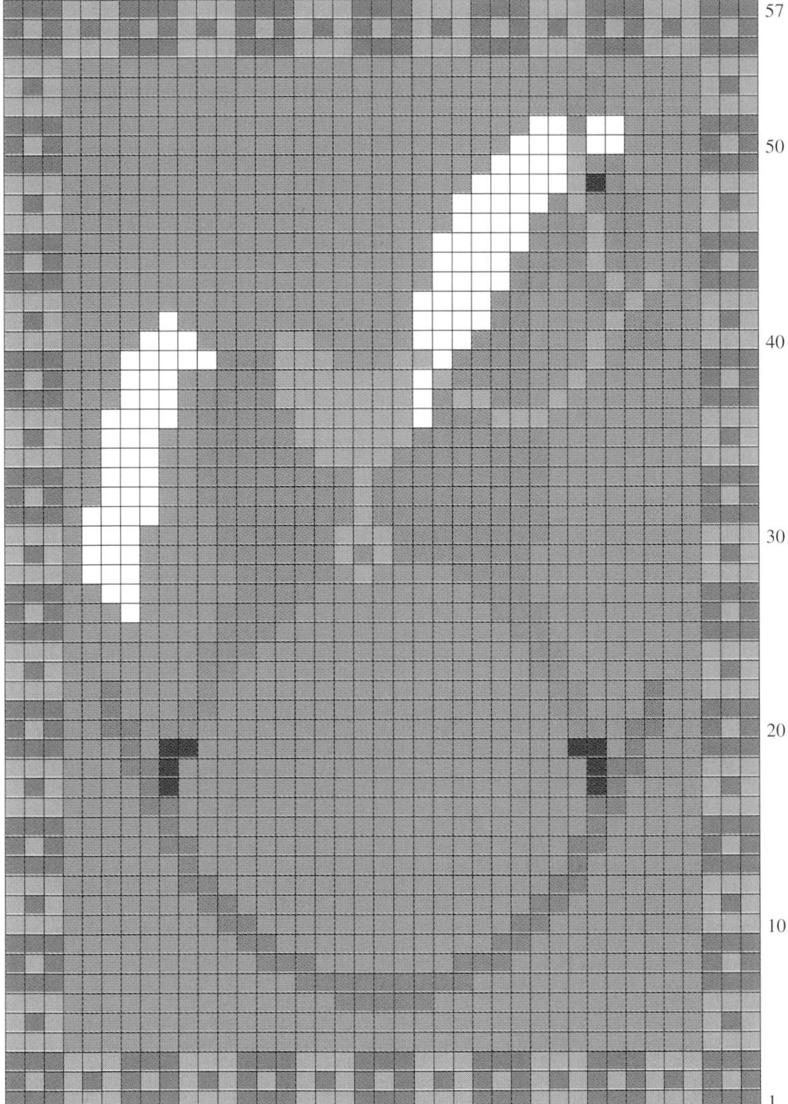

# MATINEE JACKET AND BONNET

*Pretty in pink*

*For Intermediate Knitters*

**Baby-weight yarn and light lacy stitches are a sweet reminder of old-fashioned style. Top it off with a matching bonnet with silk ribbon ties. Designed by E. J. Slayton.**

### CARDIGAN SIZES

Instructions are written for size Preemie-3 months. Changes for sizes 6, 12 and 18 months are in parentheses.

### BONNET SIZES

Instructions are written for size 3-6 months. Changes for size 12-18 months are in parentheses.

### KNITTED MEASUREMENTS

- Finished chest (buttoned) 21 (23, 25, 27)"/53 (58.5, 63.5, 68.5)cm
- Length 8¾ (9¾, 10¾, 11½)"/22.5 (24.5, 27, 29)cm
- Upper arm 7 (7½, 8, 8½)"/17.5 (19, 20, 21.5)cm

### MATERIALS

- 3 (3, 4, 4) .88oz/25g skeins (each approx 165yd/150m) of Filatura Di Crosa/Stacy Charles *Monbébé* (wool①) in #504 pink
- Two size 2 (2.5mm) circular needles, 16"/40cm long *or size to obtain gauge*
- Size 3 (3mm) circular needle, 16"/40cm long
- Stitch markers and holders
- Three ¼"/6mm buttons
- ½yd/.5m silk ribbon ⅜"/9mm wide

### GAUGE

30 sts and 40 rows to 4"/10cm over flower lace pat II using smaller needle.
*Take time to check gauge.*

### STITCH GLOSSARY

**Note** When working pats I and II on collar and bonnet, beg and end pat rows 3 and 5 with k1, rather than k2.

**Flower Lace Pattern I**
(multiple of 10 sts plus 3 on larger needles)
**Row 1 (RS)** Knit.
**Rows 2, 4 and 6** Purl.
**Rows 3 and 5** K2, *yo, k3, sl 2 sts tog, k1, pass 2 slipped sts over k1 (double dec), k3, yo, k1; rep from * , end last rep k2.
**Row 7** Knit.
**Row 8** Purl.
Rep rows 1-8 for pat I.

**Flower Lace Pattern II**
(multiple of 8 sts plus 3 on smaller needles)
**Row 1 (RS)** Knit.
**Rows 2, 4 and 6** Purl.
**Rows 3 and 5** K2, *yo, k2, double dec, k2, yo, k1; rep from *, end last rep k2.
**Row 7** Knit.
**Row 8** Purl.
Rep rows 1-8 for pat II.

### CARDIGAN

### BACK

With larger needle, loosely cast on 203 (223, 243, 263) sts. Working back and forth on circular needle, work in garter st for 5 rows. Change to pat I and work 8-row rep 4 (5, 6, 6) times; work rows 1-6 once.
**Next (dec) row** K5, *double dec, k7; rep from * end last rep k5—163 (179, 195, 211) sts.
**Next row** Purl. Change to smaller needle and work rows 1-8 of pat II once, rows 1-6 once. Piece measures approx 5¼ (6, 6¾, 7)"/13.5 (15.5, 17, 17.5)cm from beg.

**Divide for fronts and back**
**Next row (RS)** Cont in pats as established,

work 37 (41, 45, 49) sts and sl to a holder for right front; bind off 9 sts for armhole; work until there are 71 (79, 87, 95) sts for back; sl rem sts to a holder for left front.

### Armhole shaping

Working back and forth on sts for back only, cont in pat as established, AT SAME TIME, dec 1 st each side every other row 4 times—63 (71, 79, 87) sts. Work even until armhole measures 3½ (3¾, 4, 4½)"/9 (9.5, 10, 11.5)cm. Place 18 (22, 24, 28) sts each side on holders for shoulders; place rem 27 (27, 31, 31) sts on a holder for back neck.

## LEFT FRONT

Sl 46 (50, 54, 58) sts for left front back to needle, ready to work RS row. Bind off 9 sts at beg of next row for front armhole. Cont in pat as established, working armhole decs at side edge (beg of RS rows) as for back, until armhole measures 2 (2¼, 2¼, 2½)"/5 (5.5, 5.5, 6.5)cm, end with a RS row.

### Neck shaping

**Next row (WS)** Bind off 9 (9, 11, 11) sts, work to end. Cont in pat as established, AT SAME TIME, dec 1 st at neck edge every other row 6 times. When same length as back, sl rem 18 (22, 24, 28) sts to a holder.

## RIGHT FRONT

Work as for left front, reversing shaping.

## SLEEVES

With smaller needles, cast on 43 sts. Work in garter st for 5 rows, then work 8-row rep of pat II once. Change to larger needle and cont in pat as established, AT SAME TIME, inc 1 st each side (working incs on 2nd and next to last st) every 6th row 5 (7, 9, 11) times—53 (57, 61, 65) sts. Work even until piece measures 5¼ (5½, 5¾, 6)"/13.5 (14, 14.5, 15)cm from beg, end with a WS row.

### Cap shaping

Bind off 5 sts at beg of next 2 rows, dec 1 st each side every other row 3 times.

**Next row (WS)** Knit. Bind off rem 37 (41, 45, 49) sts.

## FINISHING

Block pieces to measurements. Finish shoulders using 3 needle bind off (see page 65).

### Right front edging

From RS, with larger needle, beg at lower edge, pick up and k 2 sts for every 3 rows to neck.

**Row 1 (WS)** Sl 1, k to end.

**Rows 2 and 3** Rep row 1.

**Row 4** Sl 1, k to 24 sts from end, [yo, k2tog, k8] twice, yo k2tog, k2.

**Rows 5 and 6** Rep row 1.

**Row 7** Sl 1, k to last 3 sts, k2tog, k1.

**Row 8** Sl 1, k2tog, pass sl st over k2tog, bind off rem sts purlwise.

### Left front edging

Work as for right front edging, omitting buttonholes and reversing shaping on rows 7 and 8.

### Neckband

With WS facing and larger needle, pick up and k 9 (9, 11, 11) sts across left front band, 10 (10, 12, 12) sts along neck to shoulder, k 27 (27, 31, 31) back neck sts from holder, 10 (10, 12, 12) sts from shoulder to right front band, 9 (9, 11, 11) sts across band—65 (65, 77, 77) sts.

**Next row** P, dec 2 (dec 2, inc 2, inc 2) sts evenly spaced across back—63 (63, 79, 79) sts. Set piece aside.

### Collar

With larger needle, loosely cast on 77 (77, 97, 97) sts. Work in garter st for 5 rows.

**Next row** K3, work row 1 of pat I to last 3

sts, k3. Keeping first and last 3 sts in garter st, work rows 2-8 of pat I.

**Next row** K6, *double dec, k7; rep from *, end last rep k6—63 (63, 79, 79) sts. Keeping first and last 3 sts in garter st, work rows 2-8 of pat II. Change to smaller needle. Keeping first and last 3 sts in garter st, work rem sts in St st for 3 rows. Weave collar sts to back neck sts.

### BONNET

With larger needle, loosely cast on 77 (85) sts. Change to smaller needle and work in garter st for 5 rows. Keeping first and last 3 sts in St st, rep rows 1-8 of pat II until piece measures 4¾ (5¼)"/12 (13.5)cm from beg. Bind off 25 (28) sts at beg of next 2 rows. Cont in pat as established over 27 (29) sts for crown, AT SAME TIME, *for larger size only*, work pat rows 3 and 5 as foll: K2, ssk, work in pat as established to last 4 sts, k2tog, k2. Work until crown measures 1½"/94cm less than bound-off edge, dec 1 st on last WS row.

**Next row** K2 (1), *p2, k2; rep from * end p2, k2 (1). Cont in rib until crown measures same length as bound-off edge. Break yarn, leaving sts on needle. Sew bound-off edges to sides of crown. With RS facing and larger needle, pick up and k 29 (32) sts along left edge, pm, work in rib as established across sts of crown, pm, pick up and k 29 (32) sts along right edge—84 (92) sts.

**Rows 1-3** Knit, working sts between markers in rib as established.

**Rows 4-8** Work as established, dec 1 st each end every RS row. Bind off knitwise.

### FINISHING

Cut ribbon length in half; sew one half to each front corner of bonnet.

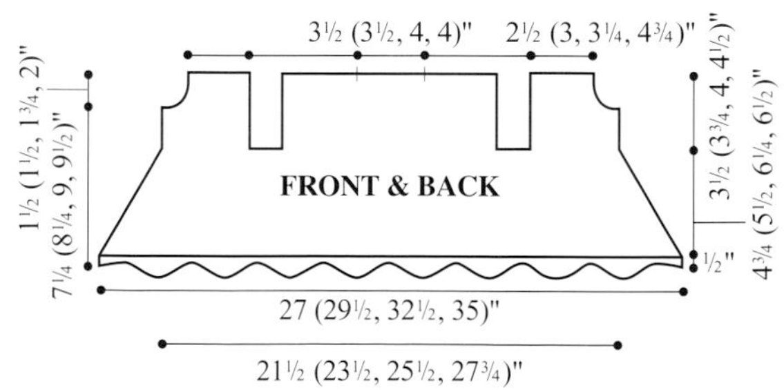


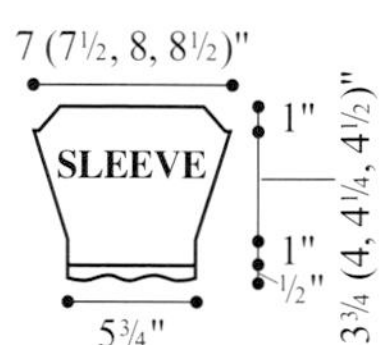

# BABY BLANKET

*Pastel patchwork*

*For Intermediate Knitters*

**Baby's first quilt. Squares are knit separately, then sewn together. Clever bind-off technique creates the dimensional braid stripes. Designed by Diane Zangl.**

### KNITTED MEASUREMENTS

38" x 38"/96.5cm x 96.5cm.

### MATERIALS

- 5 4.4oz/125g balls (each approx 256yd/233m) of Classic Elite *Provence* (cotton③) in #2601 white (MC)
- 1 ball each in #2608 blue (CC-A), #2689 pink (CC-B), #2612 yellow (CC-C) and 2691 green (CC-D)
- One pair size 4 (3.5mm) needles *or size to obtain gauge*
- Size 4 (3.5mm) circular needles, one 16"/40cm and two 36"/91cm long
- Stitch markers

### GAUGE

22 sts and 28 rows to 4"/10cm over St st using size 4 (3.5mm) needles.
*Take time to check gauge.*

### Notes

**1** Do not cut yarn when changing colors; carry unused color loosely along side.
**2** Make sure st count remains constant when picking up sts on Bound-off Braid rows.

### STITCH GLOSSARY

**Bound-off Braid**

**Row 1 (RS)** With MC, k.
**Rows 2, 4, and 6** Bind off purlwise.
**Rows 3 and 5** Pick up and k 1 st in each p "bump" behind each bound-off st
**Row 7** With CC, rep row 3.

### SQUARES

(make 10 with CC-A; 9 each with CC-B and CC-D; 8 with CC-C)

With straight needles and CC, cast on 28 sts. Beg with a purl row, work 9 rows St st, 7 rows Bound-off Braid, 7 rows St st, 7 rows Bound-off Braid, 9 rows St st. Mark each corner st. Cut CC. Change to 16"/40cm circular needle and MC.

**Edging**

K 28, *M1 at corner marker, pick up and k 28 sts along side edge; rep from *, end M1 at corner. Join, mark beg of rnds.
**Rnd 1** Bind off all sts purlwise.
**Rnd 2** Rep row 3 of Bound-off Braid, AT SAME TIME, M1 at each corner.
**Rnds 3-5** Rep rnds 1 and 2. Cut yarn, leaving a long end. Draw yarn through last lp, thread yarn into tapestry needle and weave needle under both lps of first st then back through center of last st.

### FINISHING

Foll photo and assembly diagram for placement, sew squares tog.

**Border**

With MC and both long circular needles (to accommodate large number of sts) rep rnd 2 then rnd 1 of edging 3 times. Block piece to finished measurements.

**ASSEMBLY DIAGRAM**

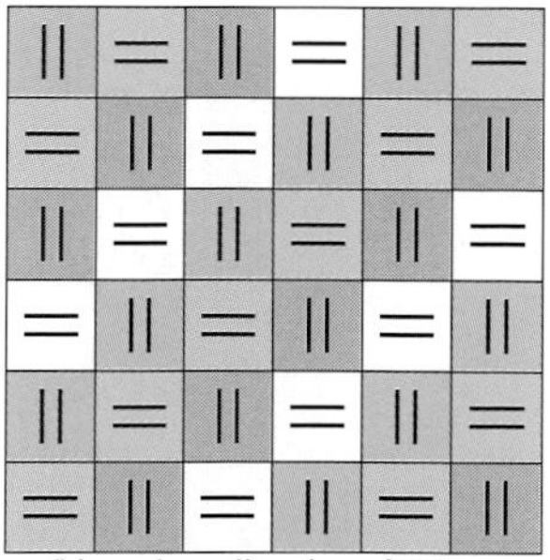

Lines show direction of stripes

# BUNTING AND CAP

*Bye, bye baby bunting*

**Plush, cozy cotton chenille is the perfect choice for baby's first bunting and matching pull-on helmet cap. Angled buttoning closure makes for easy dressing. Designed by Jil Eaton.**

#### SIZES

Instructions are written for size 3 months. Changes for 6 and 12 months are in parentheses.

#### KNITTED MEASUREMENTS

- Chest 28 (32, 34)"/71 (81, 86)cm
- Length (shoulder to foot) 22 (23½, 25)"/56 (59.5, 63.5)cm
- Upper arm 11 (12, 13)"/28 (30, 33)cm
- Hat circumference 16 (17, 18)"/40.5 (43, 45.5)cm

#### MATERIALS

- 4 (5, 5) 3½oz/100g balls (each approx 110yd/100m) of Colinette Yarns Ltd. *Hand Dyed Fandango* (cotton⑤) in #93 lapis
- One pair size 8 (5mm) needles *or size to obtain gauge*
- 1 set (5) size 8 (5mm) dpn
- Stitch holders
- Eight ⅞"/mm buttons
- One snap

#### GAUGE

14 sts and 22 rows to 4"/10cm over St st using size 8 (5mm) needles.
*Take time to check gauge.*

#### BACK

#### RIGHT LEG

Cast on 11 (14, 16) sts. Work in garter st (k every row), inc 1 st each side every other row 6 times—23 (26, 28) sts. Work even in garter st until piece measures 3"/7.5cm from beg. Cont in St st until piece measures 5½ (7, 8½)"/14 (17.5, 21.5)cm from beg, end with a WS row. Set aside.

#### LEFT LEG

Work as for right leg.

**Join legs**

**Next row (RS)** Work 23 (26, 28) sts of right leg, cast on 4 sts (crotch), work across 23 (26, 28) sts of left leg—50 (56, 60) sts. Work even until piece measures 15¾"/40cm from crotch.

**Neck shaping**

**Next row (RS)** Work 19 (22, 23) sts, join 2nd ball of yarn and bind off center 12 (12, 14) sts, work to end. Working both sides at once, bind off 2 sts from each neck edge twice. Place rem 15 (18, 19) sts each side on holder for shoulders.

#### FRONT

#### LEFT LEG

Work as for back until 1 row before leg joining.

**Next row (WS)** Cast on 8 sts, work to end—31 (34, 36) sts. Work even until piece measures 19½ (21, 22½)"/49.5 (53.5, 57)cm from beg, end with a RS row.

**Neck shaping**

**Next row (WS)** Bind off 11 (11, 12) sts (neck edge), work to end. Cont to bind off from neck edge 2 sts once and dec 1 st 3 times. When same length as back, place rem 15 (18, 19) sts on holders for shoulders.

#### RIGHT LEG

Work same as left leg until leg joining.

**Next row (RS)** Cast on 4 sts (crotch), work to end—27 (30, 32) sts.

**Note** Keep 2 sts at front edge in garter st to neck.

Work even for 3/4"/2cm, end with a WS row.

**Next (Buttonhole) row (RS)** K2, yo, k2tog, work to end. Work even for 1 1/4"/3cm more.

**Shape front angle**

**Next row (RS)** K2, inc 1 st, work to end. Cont to inc 1 st at front edge inside of garter sts, every other row 12 (17, 21) times more, every 4th row 10 (8, 6) times, AT THE SAME TIME, work a buttonhole at front edge as before every 2 1/2"/6.5cm 5 times. Work even on 50 (56, 60) sts until piece measures 19 1/2 (21, 22 1/2)"/49.5 (53.5, 57)cm from beg, end with a WS row.

**Neck shaping**

**Next row (RS)** Work 19 (22, 23) sts, join 2nd ball of yarn and bind off center 12 (12, 14), work to end. Working both sides at once, dec 1 st at each neck edge every other row 4 times. When same length as back, place rem 15 (18, 19) sts each side on holders for shoulders.

**SLEEVES**

Cast on 10 (14, 16) sts. K 1 row. Working in garter st, cast on 2 sts beg of next 10 rows—30 (34, 36) sts. Work even in garter st until piece measures 3"/7.5cm from beg. Cont in St st, inc 1 st each side every 4th row 1 (4, 5) times, every other row 3 (0, 0) times—38 (42, 46) sts. Work even until piece measures 5 1/2 (6 1/2, 8)"/14 (16.5, 20)cm from beg. Bind off.

**FINISHING**

Finish right front and back shoulders using three needle bind-off . Finish left shoulder seam in same way, leaving right front shoulder open. Place markers 5 1/2 (6, 6 1/2)"/14 (15, 16.5)cm down from shoulder seams on front and back for armholes. Sew sleeves to armhole between markers. Sew side and leg seams. Overlap right front over left front and sew crotch seams. Sew sleeve seams. Sew on buttons. Sew snap to top of left front leg.

**HAT**

**Earflaps (make 2)**

With straight needles, cast on 3 (2, 3) sts. K 1 row, then cont in garter st, inc 1 st each side *every* row 4 (5, 5) times—11 (12, 13) sts. Work even until piece measures 2 3/4 (3, 3 1/2)"/7 (7.5, 9)cm from beg.

**Body of hat**

Change to dpn and divide sts evenly over 4 needles as foll: place sts of one earflap on one needle, cast on 14 (15, 16) sts for back, place sts of 2nd earflap on needle, cast on 20 (21, 22) sts for front. Join, taking care not to twist sts on needles—56 (60, 64) sts or 14 (15, 16) sts on each needle. Cont in St st (k every rnd) for 3 (3 1/2, 4)"/7.5 (9, 10)cm. P 3 rnds.

**Shape top**

Dec 1 st at end of *every* needle every rnd (therefore 4 sts dec'd every rnd) until there are 4 sts, or 1 st on each needle. Fasten off. Draw through sts, pull tog tightly and secure.

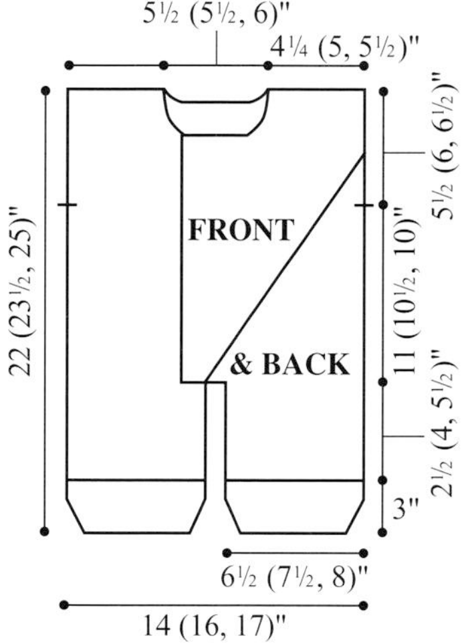


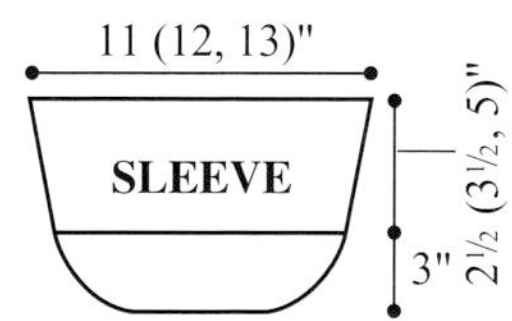


## THREE NEEDLE BIND-OFF

**1** *With RS placed together, hold pieces on two parallel needles. Insert a third needle knitwise into the first stitch of each needle, and wrap the yarn around the needle as if to knit.*

**2** *Knit these two stitches together, and slip them off the needles. *Knit the next two stitches together in the same manner.*

**3** *Slip the first stitch on the third needle over the second stitch and off the needle. Repeat from the * in Step 2 across the row until all stitches have been bound off.*

# BABY FAIR ISLE

*Northern lights*

*For Intermediate Knitters*

**Wrap up against the winter chill with a black-and-white Fair Isle cardigan. Pink stitches accent the borders; finish with a single button. Designed by Jean Guirguis.**

## SIZES

Instructions are written for size 3 months. Changes for sizes 6, 12, 18 and 24 months are in parentheses.

## KNITTED MEASUREMENTS

- Chest (buttoned) 20 (22, 23, 25, 26¾)"/50.5 (56, 58.5, 63.5, 68)cm
- Length 9½ (10½, 11½, 12½, 14)"/24 (26.5, 29, 32, 35.5)cm
- Upper arm 9 (9½, 10, 10½, 11½)"/31 (24, 25, 27, 29)cm

## MATERIALS

- 2 (2, 2, 3, 3) 1¾oz/50g balls (each approx 193yd/175m) of Dale of Norway *Baby Wool* (wool①) each in #90 black (A) and #10 white (B)
- 1 ball in #4504 pink (C)
- One pair size 3 (3mm) needles *or size to obtain gauge*
- One ½"/13mm button
- Tapestry needle

## GAUGE

30 sts and 30 rows to 4"/10cm over St st and chart II using size 3 (3mm) needles. *Take time to check gauge.*

### Notes

**1** When changing colors, twist yarns on WS to prevent holes. Carry yarn not in use loosely across WS of work.

**2** Work charts in St st.

## BACK

With A, cast on 75 (83, 87, 95, 99) sts. P 1 row on RS.

### Beg chart I

**Row 1 (WS)** Reading chart from left to right, work 4-st rep 18 (20, 21, 23, 24) times, work last 3 sts once. Cont in pat as established through row 5. With A, p next row on RS.

### Beg chart II

**Row 1 (WS)** Reading chart from left to right, work 6-st rep 12 (13, 14, 15, 16) times, work last 3 (5, 3, 5, 3) sts once. Cont in pat as established, rep rows 1-8, until piece measures 9½ (10½, 11½, 12½, 14)"/24 (26.5, 29, 32, 35.5)cm from beg. Bind off.

## LEFT FRONT

With A, cast on 45 (49, 51, 55, 58) sts. P 1 row on RS.

### Beg chart I

Reading chart from left to right, work 4-st rep 11 (12, 12, 13, 14) times, work last 1 (1, 3, 3, 2) sts once. Cont in pat as established through row 5. With A, p next row on RS.

### Beg chart II

**Row 1 (WS)** Reading chart from left to right, work 6-st rep 7 (8, 8, 9, 9) times, work last 3 (1, 3, 1, 4) sts once. Cont in pat as established until piece measures 5½ (6½, 7, 8, 9)"/14 (16.5, 17.5, 20.5, 23)cm from beg, end with a RS row.

### Neck shaping

**Next row (RS)** Work to last 2 sts, k2tog. Cont to dec 1 st at neck edge every row 14 (16, 14, 14, 14) times more, then every other row 6 (5, 8, 8, 10) times—24 (27, 28, 32, 33) sts. Work even until same length as back. Bind off rem sts for shoulder.

### RIGHT FRONT

Work to correspond to left front, reversing shaping.

### SLEEVES

With A, cast on 45 (45, 49, 49, 49) sts. P 1 row on RS.

**Beg chart I**

Reading chart from left to right, work 4-st rep 11 (11, 12, 12, 12) times, work 1 st after rep. Cont in pat as established through row 5. With A, p next row on RS.

**Beg chart II**

**Row 1 (WS)** Reading chart from left to right, work 6-st rep 7 (7, 8, 8, 8) times, work last 3 (3, 1, 1, 1) sts once. Cont in pat as established, AT SAME TIME, inc 1 st each side (working inc sts into pat) every other row 7 (9, 8, 7, 1) times, every 4th row 4 (4, 5, 8, 18) times—67 (71, 75, 79, 87) sts. Work even until piece measures 5½ (6, 6½, 7¾, 11½)"/14 (15.5, 16.5, 19.5, 29)cm from beg. Bind off all sts.

### FINISHING

Block pieces. Sew shoulder seams. Place markers 4½ (4¾, 5, 5¼, 5¾)"/11.5 (12, 12.5, 13.5, 14.5)cm down from shoulders on front and back. Sew top of sleeves between markers. Sew side and sleeve seams.

**Neckband**

With right side facing and A, beg at right front edge, pick up and k 169 (185, 201, 217, 245) sts evenly along right front, back neck and left front edge. K next row on WS. Work chart 1, working 4-st rep 42 (46, 50, 54, 61) times, then work first st once more. Cont as established through chart row 5. Bind off knitwise with A on WS. With A, make a 2"/5cm button loop and attach to right front band at beg of neck shaping. Sew button on opposite loop at 2½"/6cm in from left front edge.

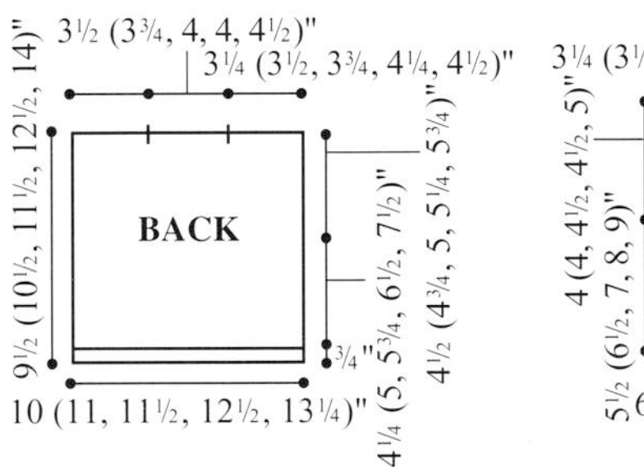


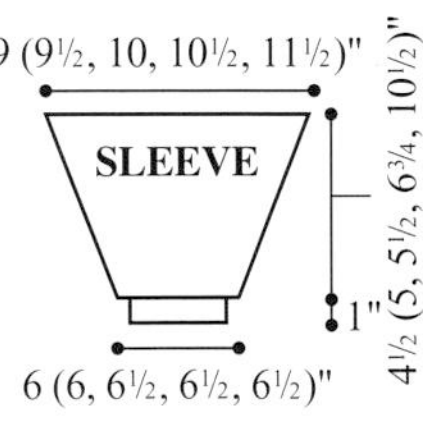

## Color key

■ Black (A)

□ White (B)

▒ Pink (C)

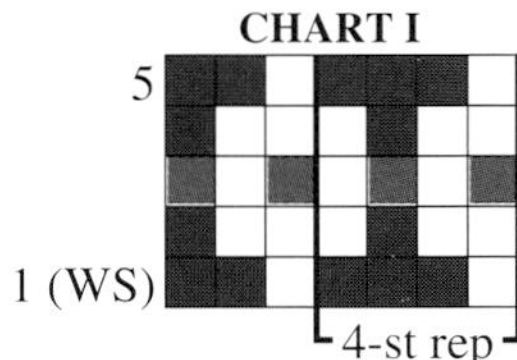


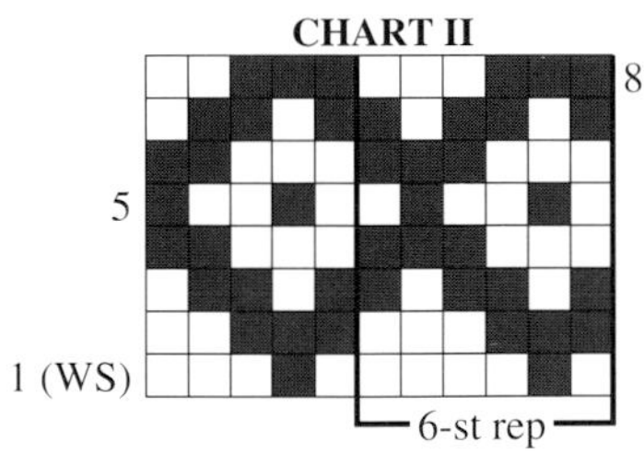

# SILK DRESS

*Playing dress-up*

*For Intermediate Knitters*

**A little luxury. Seed-stitch and cabled bodice is stitched to a softly-gathered silk duppioni skirt, then topped with a Peter Pan collar. A buttoned back opening completes this special dress, designed by Elsie Faulconer.**

### SIZES

Instructions are written for size 9-12 months. Changes for size 18-24 months are in parentheses.

### KNITTED MEASUREMENTS

- Chest 19 (25½)"/48 (64.5)cm
- Upper arm 6¼ (7½)"/16 (19)cm

### MATERIALS

- 3 1¾oz/50g skeins (each approx 156yd/144m) of Lang/Berroco *La-Se-Ta* (silk②) in #7619 pink
- One pair size 2 (2.5mm) needles *or size to obtain gauge*
- Cable needle (cn)
- Three ⅝"/15mm buttons
- 1yd/1m silk fabric 45"/114cm wide (Fabric by Angus International; *Mystique Plaid* #284)
- Matching sewing thread

### GAUGE

37 sts and 48 rows to 4"/10cm over cable pat and seed st using size 2 (2.5mm) needles. *Take time to check gauge.*

### STITCH GLOSSARY

#### Cable Pattern

(over 8 sts)

**Row 1 (WS)** K2, p4, k2.

**Row 2** P2, k4, p2.

**Row 3** Rep row 1.

**Row 4** P2, sl 2 sts to cn and hold to *front*, k2, k2 from cn, p2.

Rep rows 1-4 for cable pat.

#### Seed Stitch

**Row 1 (RS)** *K1, p1; rep from *.

**Row 2** P the knit sts, and k the purl sts.

Rep row 2 for seed st.

### BODICE FRONT

Cast on 89 (119) sts. Work in k1, p1 rib for 4 rows.

**Next row (WS)** Working row 1 of pats, work seed st over 2 sts, *p1, cable pat over 8 sts, p1, seed st over 5 sts; rep from * end last rep seed st over 2 sts.

**Next row** Working row 2 of pats, work seed st over 2 sts, *k1 tbl, cable pat over 8 sts, k1 tbl, seed st over 5 sts; rep from * end last rep seed st over 2 sts. Cont in pats as established, until piece measures 1½ (2½)"/4 (6.5)cm from beg, end with a WS row.

#### Armhole shaping

**Note** Omit working cable cross when too few sts rem.

Bind off 3 sts at beg of next 2 rows, 2 sts at beg of next 2 rows, dec 1 st each side every other row 2 (3) times—75 (103) sts. Cont in pats until armhole measures 2½ (3)"/6.5 (7.5)cm, end with a WS row.

#### Neck shaping

**Next row** Work 31 (43) sts, join a 2nd ball of yarn and bind off center 13 (17) sts, work to end. Working both sides at once, bind off 3 sts from each neck edge 1 (2) times, 2 sts 3 times, dec 1 st each side every other row twice. Work even until armholes measure 3½ (4¼)"/9 (10.5)cm. Bind off rem 20 (29) sts each side for shoulders.

### RIGHT BACK

Cast on 47 (62) sts. Work rib as for front.

**Next row (WS)** Working row 1 of pats, work seed st over 5 sts, *p1, cable pat over

8 sts, p1, seed st over 5 sts; rep from *, end last rep seed st over 2 sts.

**Next row** Working row 2 of pats, work seed st over 2 sts, *k1 tbl, cable pat over 8 sts, k1 tbl, seed st over 5 sts; rep from * to end. Cont in pats as established and when piece measures same length as front to armhole, shape armhole at side edge only (beg of RS rows) as for front. Cont in pats until same length as front to shoulder. Bind off rem 40 (54) sts. Place markers for 3 buttons along center back, the first one ½"/1.5cm below neck edge, the last one 1½ (2)"/4 (5)cm above lower edge, and one centered between.

### LEFT BACK

Work as for right back, reversing shaping and working a buttonhole opposite markers as foll: Work 2 sts, bind off 2 sts, work to end.

**Buttonhole row (RS)** On the foll row, cast on 2 sts over bound-off sts.

### SLEEVES

Cast on 59 (69) sts. Work rib as for back.

**Next row (WS)** Working row 1 of pats, work seed st over 2 (7) sts, *p1, cable pat over 8 sts, p1, seed st over 5 sts; rep from * end last rep seed st over 2 (7) sts. Cont in pats as established until piece measures 1 (1½)"/2.5 (4)cm from beg, end with a WS row.

**Cap shaping**

Bind off 3 sts at beg of next 2 rows, 2 sts at beg of next 8 (10) rows. Bind off rem 37 (43) sts.

### FINISHING

Sew shoulder seams. Set in sleeves. Sew side and sleeve seams. Overlap left center back seed st edge over right back and tack in place. Sew on buttons.

**Skirt**

From fabric, cut 1 (2) skirt pieces each 12 (16)" x 45 (28)"/30.5 (40.5)cm x 114 (71)cm. With RS tog and using a ⅝"/ 15mm seam allowance, *for smaller size* sew back seam, *for larger size* sew 2 side seams. Gather one long edge of skirt, adjust gathers to fit; hand-sew to lower edge of bodice. Press ¼"/6mm to WS along rem long edge of skirt, then hem to desired length.

From rem fabric, cut 2 pairs of collars and 2 bias strips each 1" x 6"/2.5cm x 15cm. With RS tog and a ¼"/6mm seam allowance, sew pairs of collars, leaving open at neck edge. Turn to RS. With RS tog and using a ¼"/6mm allowance, sew long edge of bias strip to raw edge of collar. Press ¼"/6mm to WS along rem long edge of bias and sew to inside of bodice neck, easing to fit and turning in raw ends of strip.

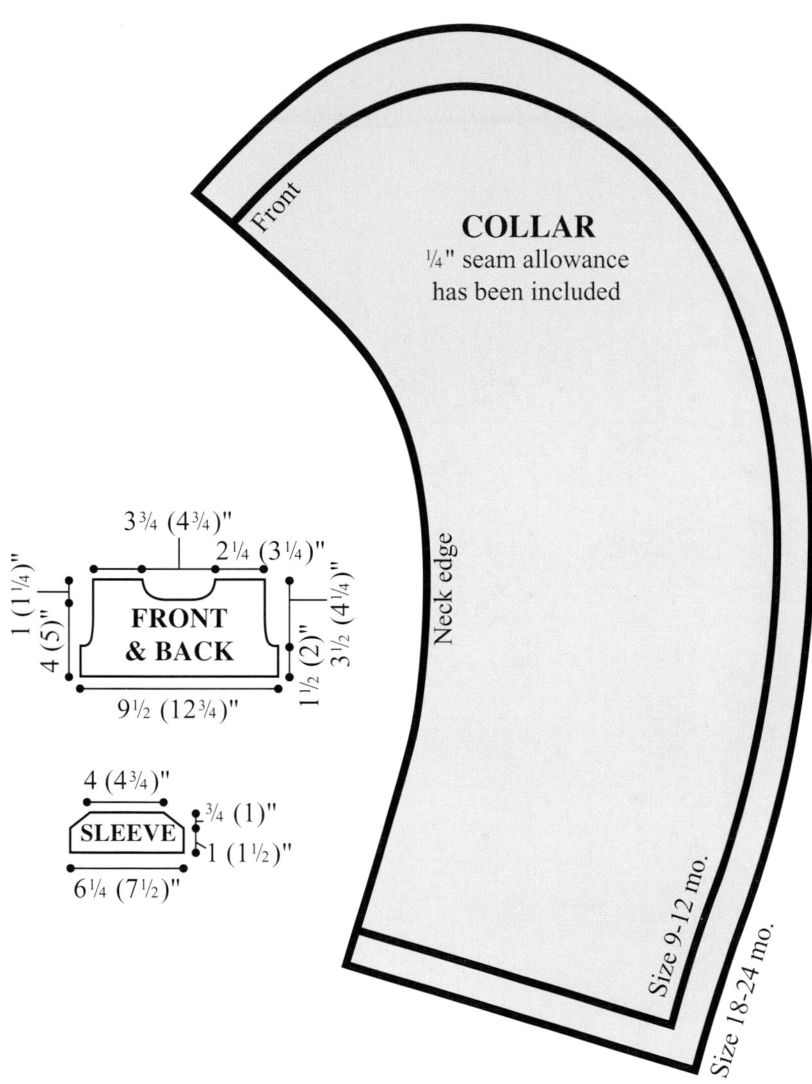
COLLAR
¼" seam allowance
has been included
Front
Neck edge
Size 9-12 mo.
Size 18-24 mo.
3¾ (4¾)"
2¼ (3¼)"
1 (1¼)"
4 (5)"
3½ (4¼)"
1½ (2)"
FRONT
& BACK
9½ (12¾)"
4 (4¾)"
¾ (1)"
SLEEVE
1 (1½)"
6¼ (7½)"

# COAT-DRESS AND BONNET

*From an English garden*

*For Intermediate Knitters*

**Perfect for a stroll in the park with the nanny. Pretty coat in all-over Fair Isle has a striped yoke and garter edges. The bonnet is finished with a charming ruffle to frame baby's face. Designed by Sasha Kagan.**

### SIZES

Instructions are for written for size 6 months. Changes for sizes 12, 18 and 24 months are in parentheses.

### KNITTED MEASUREMENTS

**Coat**

- Chest 23¾ (25, 26¼, 27½)"/60.5 (63.5, 66.5, 69.5)cm
- Length 15½ (16½, 17½, 18¼)"/39.5 (42, 44.5, 46.5)cm
- Upper arm 6½ (7¾, 7¾, 9)"/16.5 (19.5, 19.5, 23)cm

**Bonnet**

- Front edge width 11½ (13, 14, 15½)"/ 29 (33, 35.5, 39.5)cm

### MATERIALS

- 2 (3, 3, 3) .88oz/25g balls (each approx 108yd/100m) of Rowan *Donegal Lambswool Tweed* (wool②) in #469 oatmeal (A)
- 1 ball in #477 tarragon (B), #481 leaf (C)
- 2 (2, 2, 3) .80oz/25g balls (each approx 72yd/67m) of Rowan *Lightweight DK* (wool②) in #501 bluebell (D) #95 pink (E)
- 1 1¾oz/50g balls (each approx 184yd/170m) of Rowan *Botany* (wool②) in #559 snowdrop (F), #570 lilac ice (G), #559 avocado (H), #541 primrose (I)
- One pair each sizes 2 and 4 (2.5 and 3.5 mm) needles *or size to obtain gauge*
- 5 stitch holders
- Tapestry needle
- Bobbins
- 9 (9, 10, 10) ⅜"/10mm buttons

### GAUGE

31 sts and 35 rows to 4"/10cm over St st and Fair Isle chart using larger needles.
*Take time to check gauge.*

**Notes**

**1)** Coat is worked in one piece to armhole, then fronts and back are worked separately to yoke. Yoke is worked across all sts to neck.
**2)** When changing colors, twist yarns on WS to prevent holes in work.
**3)** Carry background colors across back of work. Use individual bobbins for each flower.
**4)** Duplicate st center of flowers with I.

### STITCH GLOSSARY

**Seed Stitch**

**Row 1 (RS)** *K1, p1; rep from * to end.
**Row 2** K the purl sts and p the knit sts.
Rep row 2 for seed st.

**Stripe Pattern**

Working in garter st, work *2 rows A, 2 row F; rep from * (4 rows) for stripe pat.

### BODY

With smaller needles and A, cast on 180 (190, 200, 210) sts. Work in seed st for 8 rows. Change to larger needles. Work in St st and Fair Isle chart until 80 (88, 96, 104) rows of chart have been worked. Piece measures approx 9¾ (10¾, 11¾, 12½)"/24.5 (27, 30, 31.5)cm from beg.

**Divide for fronts and back**

**Next row (RS)** Work 40 (42, 45, 47) sts and place on holder for right front, bind off 10 sts for underarm, work until there are 80 (86, 90, 96) sts on RH needle and place on holder for back, bind off 10 sts, work last 40 (42, 45, 47) sts for left front. Cont on left front sts only as foll:

### LEFT FRONT

**Row 1 (WS)** Purl.

**Row 2** Ssk, k to end.

Rep last 2 rows 12 times more—27 (29, 32, 34) sts. P next row and place sts on holder.

### RIGHT FRONT

Place sts from right front holder onto needle.

**Row 1 (WS)** Purl.

**Row 2** K to last 2 sts, k2tog.

Rep last 2 rows and complete to correspond to left front—27 (29, 32, 34) sts.

### BACK

Place sts from back holder onto needle.

**Row 1 (WS)** Purl.

**Row 2** Ssk, k to last 2 sts, k2tog.

Rep last 2 rows until same length as front—54 (60, 64, 70) sts. Place sts on holder.

### SLEEVES

With smaller needles and A, cast on 30 (30, 32, 34) sts. Work in seed st for 8 rows, inc 20 (30, 28, 36) sts evenly across last row—50 (60, 60, 70) sts. Change to larger needles. Work in St st and Fair Isle chart, beg row 9 (9, 1, 1), until 40 (48, 48, 56) rows of chart have been worked. Piece measures approx 5¼(6¼, 6¼, 7¼)"/13.5 (16, 16, 18.5)cm from beg.

#### Raglan shaping

Bind off 5 sts at beg of next 2 rows, then dec 1 st each side every other row as for back 13 times—14 (24, 24, 34) sts. Place sts on holder. There is a total of 136 (166, 176, 206) sts on holders.

### YOKE

Cont in garter st and stripe pat as foll:

**Row 1 (RS)** With RS facing and larger needles, k across sts from right front holder, first sleeve holder, back holder, 2nd sleeve holder and left front holder as foll: K1 (1, 0, 0), *k2tog, k1; rep from *, end k0 (0, k2tog, k2tog)—91 (111, 117, 137) sts.

**Rows 2-4** Knit.

**Row 5** K6 (5, 8, 7) sts, *k2tog, k9; rep from *, end last rep k6 (5, 8, 7) sts—83 (101, 107, 125) sts.

**Rows 6-9** Knit.

**Row 10** K5 (4, 7, 6) sts, *k2tog, k8; rep from *, end last rep k6 (5, 8, 7) sts—75 (91, 97, 113) sts.

**Rows 11-14** Knit.

**Row 15** K5 (4, 7, 6) sts, *k2tog, k7; rep from *, end last rep k5 (4, 7, 6) sts—67 (81, 87, 101) sts.

**Rows 16-19** Knit.

**Row 20** K4 (3, 6, 5) sts, *k2tog, k6; rep from *, end last rep k5 (4, 7, 6) sts—59 (71, 77, 89) sts.

**Rows 21-23** Knit.

**Row 24** K4 (3, 6, 5) sts, *k2tog, k5; rep from *, end k2tog, k2 (1, 4, 3) sts, k2tog—50 (60, 66, 76) sts.

Change to smaller needles and A. Work in seed st for 4 rows. Bind off.

### FINISHING

#### Buttonband

With RS facing, smaller needles and A, pick up and k 114 (120, 126, 134) sts evenly along left front edge. Work in seed st for 6 rows. Bind off.

#### Buttonhole band

Work as for buttonband along right front edge, for 3 rows.

**Next (buttonhole) row (RS)** Work 4 sts, [yo, k2tog, work 11 (12, 11, 12) sts] 8 (8, 9, 9) times, yo, k2tog, k4 (2, 3, 2) sts.

Work 2 more rows in seed st. Bind off.
Sew buttons opposite buttonholes.
With tapestry needle, work Duplicate st with I at center of each flower.
Sew raglan and sleeve seams.

### BONNET

With smaller needles and A, cast on 180 (200, 220, 240) sts. [K 2 rows A, k 2 rows F] twice.

**Dec row (RS)** With A, k2tog across—90 (100, 110, 120) sts.

Beg with a p row, work in St st for 3 (5, 7, 9) rows. Change to larger needles. Work in St st and Fair Isle chart until 24 rows of chart have been worked. Place marker at beg and end of row. Cont in St st with A only for 10 (14, 18, 22) rows.

**Crown shaping**

**Row 1 (RS)** *K2tog, k8; rep from * to end—81 (90, 99, 108) sts.

**Row 2 and all WS rows** Purl.

**Row 3** *K7, k2tog; rep from * to end—72 (80, 88, 96) sts.

Cont in this way to dec 9 (10, 11, 12) sts every RS row, until 9 (10, 11, 12) sts rem. Cut yarn leaving an end for sewing. Thread end through rem sts and draw tightly to close.

**Ties**

With smaller needles and A, cast on 230 (230, 250, 250) sts. K 2 rows A, k 2 rows F, k 1 row A. With A bind off purlwise.

### FINISHING

Sew back seam to marked row.
Fold ties in half to find center. Pin center to seam. Sew upper edge of ties to lower edge of bonnet, from center to front edge of ruffle.

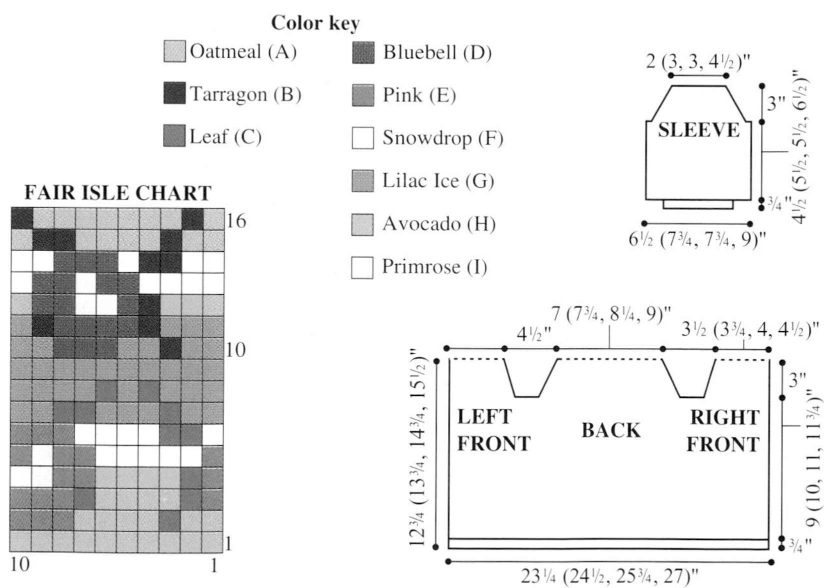

# JOGGING SUIT

*Track star*

*For Intermediate Knitters*

**Racing stripes for your little champion. Sweatshirt and pants knit in super-comfy cotton bouclé sport an intarsia number and ribbed cuffs. Designed by Teva Durham.**

## SIZES

Instructions are written for size 6 months. Changes for sizes 12, 18 and 24 months are in parentheses.

## KNITTED MEASUREMENTS

### Pants

- Waist 19 (21, 22, 23½)"/48 (53, 55.5, 59.5)cm
- Inseam 7 (8, 9, 10)"/17.5 (20, 22.5, 25)cm

### Top

- Chest 24 (26, 30, 31)"/61 (66, 76, 78.5)cm
- Length 10¼ (12, 13¼, 15)"/26 (30.5, 33.5, 38)cm
- Upper arm 9 (10½, 11¾, 13)"/22.5 (26.5, 29.5, 33)cm

## MATERIALS

### Pants

- 2 (2, 3, 3) 1¾oz/50g skeins (each approx 127yd/117m) of Pingouin *Alizé* (acrylic/cotton③) in #010 red (MC)
- 1 skein in #001 white (A)
- One pair each sizes 1 and 4 (2.25 and 3.5mm) needles *or size to obtain gauge*
- Stitch holders
- 1yd/1m length of ½"/13mm wide elastic

### Top

- 3 (3, 4, 4) 1¾oz/50g skeins (each approx 127yd/117m) of Pingouin *Alizé* (acrylic/cotton③) in #010 red (MC)
- 1 skein in #001 white (A)
- One pair each sizes 1 and 4 (2.25 and 3.5mm) needles *or size to obtain gauge*
- Stitch holders
- One ⅝"/15mm button

## GAUGE

21 sts and 26 rows to 4"/10cm over St st using larger needles.
*Take time to check gauge.*

## PANTS

### LEG

With larger needles and MC, cast on 40 (46, 48, 50) sts. Change to smaller needles. Work in k1, p1 rib for ¾"/2cm, end with a RS row. Change to larger needles.

**Next row (WS)** K, inc 8 (8, 10, 12) sts evenly spaced—48 (54, 58, 62) sts.

**Next row (RS)** K20 (23, 25, 27) MC, k3 A, k2 MC, k3 A, k20 (23, 25, 27) MC. Cont in St st with colors as established, AT SAME TIME, inc 1 st each side every 3rd row 8 times, every 4th row 3 (4, 5, 7) times—70 (78, 84, 92) sts. Work even until piece measures 7 (8, 9, 10)"/17.5 (20, 22.5, 25)cm from beg, end with a WS row.

### Crotch shaping

Bind off 3 (3, 3, 4) sts at beg of next 2 rows, 2 sts at beg of next 2 rows. Dec 1 st each side every other row 2 (2, 2, 3) times—56 (64, 70, 74) sts. Work even until piece measures 13 (14, 16, 18)"/33 (35.5, 40, 45.5)cm from beg, end with a WS row, dec 0 (0, 4, 4) sts evenly across last row. Sl rem 56 (64, 66, 70) sts to a holder.

Work a 2nd leg in same way.

## FINISHING

Block pieces to measurements. From RS, with smaller needles and MC, work across sts on holders as foll: k to last st on first holder, k last st of first holder tog with first st of 2nd holder, k across sts on 2nd holder—111 (127, 131, 139) sts. Work in k1, p1 rib for 3/4"/2cm, end with a RS row. K next row on WS for turning ridge. Work in k1, p1 rib for 3/4"/2cm. Bind off in rib. Sew inner leg seams. Sew crotch seam. Fold rib to WS along turning ridge and sew in place, leaving an opening for elastic. Insert elastic, adjust to fit, sew ends of elastic tog. Sew opening closed.

## TOP

### BACK

With larger needles and MC, cast on 57 (63, 74, 76) sts. Change to smaller needles. Work in k1, p1 rib for 3/4"/2cm, end with a RS row. Change to larger needles.

**Next row (WS)** K, inc 6 (6, 5, 5) sts evenly spaced—63 (69, 79, 81) sts. Work in St st until piece measures 5 1/4 (6 1/2, 7, 8)"/13 (16.5, 17.5, 20)cm from beg, end with a WS row.

#### Raglan armhole shaping

Bind off 4 sts at beg of next 2 rows. Dec 1 st each side every other row 14 (15, 15, 22) times, *every* row 2 (4, 8, 0) times—23 (23, 25, 29) sts, AT SAME TIME, when piece measures 8 3/4 (10, 11 1/4, 13)"/22 (25, 28.5, 33)cm from beg, end with a WS row.

#### Divide for placket

**Next row (RS)** Work to center st, join a 2nd ball of yarn and bind off center st, work to end. Working both sides at once, cont in St st, working raglan decs as established, until piece measures 10 1/4 (12, 13 1/4, 15)"/26 (30, 33.5, 38)cm from beg. Bind off rem 11 (11, 12, 14) sts each side.

### FRONT

Work as for back until piece measures 2 (3, 3 1/2, 4 1/2)"/5, (7.5, 8.5, 11)cm from beg, end with a WS row.

#### Beg number chart

**Next row (RS)** Work 22 (25, 30, 31) sts, work 19 sts chart, work to end. Cont chart as established through row 35, then cont with MC only, AT SAME TIME, when same length as back to raglan armhole, work shaping as for back until same length as back to placket, end with a WS row.

#### Neck shaping

**Next row (RS)** Cont armhole shaping, work to center 13 (13, 15, 19) sts, join a 2nd ball of yarn and bind off 13 (13, 15, 19) sts, work to end. Working both sides at once, bind off from each neck 2 sts once, dec 1 st every other row 3 times. Cont working raglan decs as established until 4 sts rem, end with a RS row.

**Next row** P2tog twice.

**Next row** K2tog, end off.

### SLEEVES

With larger needles and MC, cast on 24 (28, 34, 38) sts. Change to smaller needles. Work in k1, p1 rib for 3/4"/2cm, end with a RS row. Change to larger needles.

**Next row (WS)** K, inc 6 sts evenly spaced—30 (34, 40, 44) sts.

**Next row (RS)** K 11 (13, 16, 18) MC, k3 A, k2 MC, k3 A, k 11 (13, 16, 18) MC. Cont in St st with colors as established, AT SAME TIME, inc 1 st each side every other row 7 (8, 5, 3) times, every 4th row 2 (3, 6, 9) times—48 (56, 62, 68) sts. When piece measures 5 1/4 (6, 7, 8 1/4)"/13 (15, 17.5, 20.5)cm from beg, end with a WS row.

#### Raglan shaping

Bind off 4 sts at beg of next 2 rows. Dec 1 st each side every other row 13 (14, 16, 20) times, *every* row 4 (6, 6, 4) times.

Bind off rem 6 (8, 10, 12) sts.

**FINISHING**

Block pieces to measurements. Sew raglan seams.

**Neckband**

With RS facing, smaller needles and MC, beg at left back, pick up and k 74 (74, 76, 82) sts around neck, cast on 5 sts (for button tab)—79 (79, 81, 87) sts. Work back and forth in k1, p1 rib for 3 rows.

**Next row** Work to last 4 sts, k2tog, yo, work to end. Work 3 more rows in rib. Bind off 5 sts at beg of next 2 rows. Cont in rib until neckband measures 1½"/3.5cm. Bind off loosely in rib.

Sew side and sleeve seams. Sew on button.

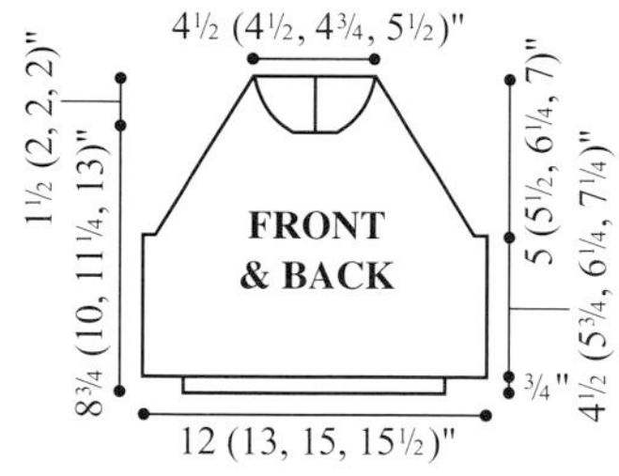


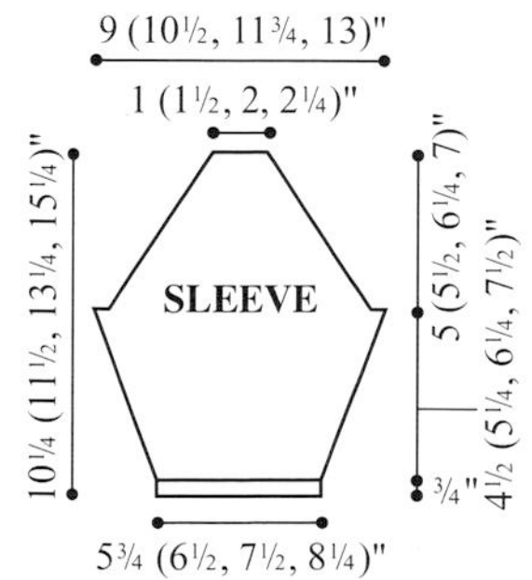


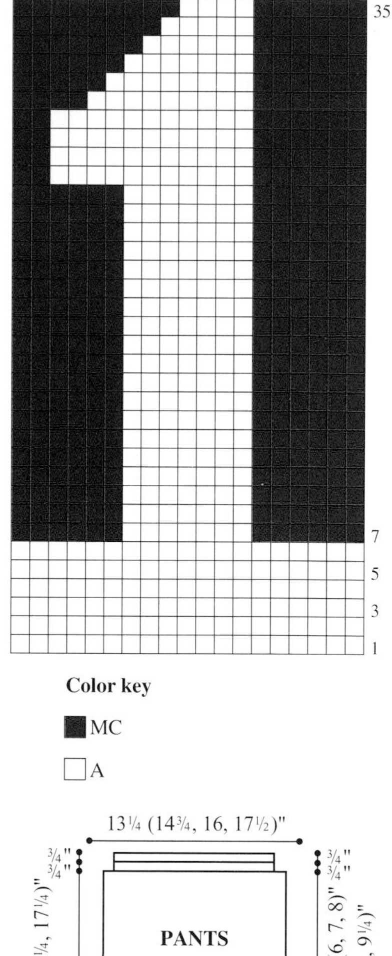


**Color key**

MC

A

# SLEEVELESS ROMPER

*Beach baby, beach baby*

**Cool stripes are set for the seashore. Rolled edges and easy-access buttoning at the legs and shoulders are sure to make this a summer favorite. Designed by Victoria Mayo.**

SIZES

Instructions are written for size 6 months. Changes for 12, 18 and 24 months are in parentheses.

KNITTED MEASUREMENTS

- Chest 23 (24, 26, 27½)"/58.5 (61, 66, 69.5)cm
- Length 14¼ (15,16¼, 17¼)"/36 (38, 41, 44)cm

MATERIALS

- 2 (2, 2, 3) 1¾oz/50g balls (each approx 110yd/100m) of Trendsetter Yarns *Elba* (cotton②) each in #512 aqua (A) and #001 white (B)
- 1 ball in #8 green (C)
- Size 6 (4mm) needles *or size to obtain gauge*
- Eight ½"/13mm buttons

GAUGE

24 sts and 36 rows to 4"/10cm over St st using size 6 (4mm) needles.
*Take time to check gauge.*

STITCH GLOSSARY

**Dec 2 (RS)**

Sl next 2 sts knitwise to RH needle, k next st, then pass 2 slipped sts, one at a time, over k st.

**Dec 2 (WS)**

Sl next 2 sts purlwise to RH needle, p next st, then pass 2 slipped sts, one at a time, over p st.

**Stripe pat**

*2 rows B, 2 rows A; rep from * (4 rows) for stripe pat.

BACK

**Left leg**

With C, cast on 32 (34, 36, 39) sts. Work in St st for 4 rows. Cont in St st and stripe pat, inc 1 st at beg of every RS row (inside leg seam) 10 times—42 (44, 46, 49) sts. Work even until piece measures 2¾ (2¾, 3¼, 3¼)"/7 (7, 8.5, 8.5)cm from beg, end with a RS row. Set aside.

**Right leg**

Work as for left leg, reversing leg shaping.

**Leg joining**

**Next row (WS)** P41 (43, 45, 48) sts of left leg, p last st of left leg tog with first st of right leg, p to end—83 (87, 91, 97) sts.

**Next row (RS)** K40 (42, 44, 47), dec 2, k to end. Cont to dec 2 sts over center 3 sts *every* row 4 (5, 3, 4) times more, every other row twice—69 (71, 79, 83) sts. Work even until piece measures 7 (7½, 8, 8½)"/18 (19, 20.5, 21.5)cm above leg joining.

**Armhole shaping**

Bind off 3 (3, 4, 4) sts at beg of next 2 rows, 2 sts at beg of next 4 (2, 4, 4) rows, dec 1 st each side every other row 6 times—43 (49, 51, 55) sts. Work even until armhole measures 3½ (3¾, 4, 4½)"/9 (9.5, 10, 11.5)cm, end with a WS row.

**Neck shaping**

**Next row (RS)** Work 18 (20, 20, 21) sts, join 2nd ball of yarn and bind off center 7 (9, 11, 13) sts, work to end. Working both sides at once, bind off 5 sts from each neck edge once, 4 sts once. Work 3 rows even on 9 (11, 11, 12) sts each side. Cont in k1, p1 rib with B for 4 row. Bind off in rib.

## FRONT

Work as for back until armhole measures 2½ (2½, 2½, 3)"/6.5 (6.5, 6.5, 7.5)cm, end with a WS row.

### Neck shaping

**Next row (RS)** Work 19 (21, 21, 22) sts, join 2nd ball of yarn and bind off center 5 (7, 9, 11) sts, work to end. Working both sides at once, bind off 3 sts from each neck edge once, 2 sts 3 times, 1 st once—9 (11, 11, 12) sts. Work even until same length as back. Cont in k1, p1 rib with B for 1 row.

**Next (buttonhole) row** Rib 1 (2, 2, 2), yo, k2tog, rib 3 (3, 3, 4), yo, k2tog, rib to end. Rib 2 rows more. Bind off in rib.

## FINISHING

Block pieces to measurements. Sew side seams.

### Leg bands

With RS facing and C, pick up and k 39 (39, 45, 45) sts along inside of legs on back. Work in k1, p1 rib for 5 rows. Bind off in rib. Work front legs as for back, working buttonholes on 3rd row as foll: rib 4, [yo, k2tog, rib 8 (10)] 3 times, yo, k2tog, rib to end. Complete as for back band.

### Back neckband

With RS facing and C, pick up and k 38 (42, 46, 50) sts evenly along back neck. Work in k1, p1 rib for 3 rows. Cont in St st for 4 rows. Bind off. Work front neckband in same way, picking up 44 (48, 52, 56) sts. Work armhole bands in same way, picking up 60 (64, 68, 74) sts. Sew on buttons.

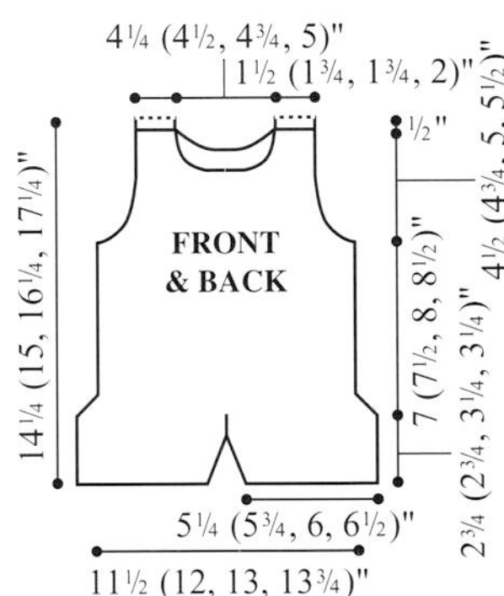

# BRITISH BABY SET

*Cuddled in cables*

*For Intermediate Knitters*

**Traditional three-piece set worked in eyelet cables is accented with Fair Isle bands. Buttoned jacket ends in a flared skirt; pants have a comfortable elastic waist. It's all topped off with a pull-on cap. Designed by Kirsten Cowan.**

### SIZES

Instructions are written for size Newborn. Changes for sizes 6, 12, 18 and 24 months are in parentheses.

### KNITTED MEASUREMENTS

**Cardigan**

- Chest 20½ (22¾, 24¼, 26, 27½)"/52 (58, 61.5, 66, 70)cm
- Length 11½ (12½, 13½, 14½, 15½)"/29 (31.5, 34.5, 37, 39.5)cm

**Pants**

- Waist 17 (19, 21, 21, 23)"/43 (48.5, 53.5, 53.5, 58.5)cm
- Length 12½ (13½, 14½, 15½, 16½)"/31.5 (34.5, 37, 39.5, 42)cm

**Hat** (Sizes Small, Medium and Large)

- Head circumference 15 (16½, 17½)"/38 (42, 44.5)cm

### MATERIALS

- 7 (8, 8, 9, 10) 1¾oz balls (each approx 132yd/120m) of Lane Borgosesia *7 Settembre* (wool③) in #90099 ivory (A)
- 1 ball each in #41256 red (B), #41249 green (C), #41254 navy (D), #41248 teal (E)
- One pair each sizes 3 and 5 (3 and 3.75mm) needles *or size to obtain gauge*
- Three stitch holders
- Tapestry needle
- Three ½"/13mm buttons
- 18 (20, 22, 22, 24)"/45.5 (50.5, 56, 56, 61)cm length of 1"/2.5cm wide elastic

### GAUGES

- 27 sts and 31 rows to 4"/10cm over cable pat slightly stretched using larger needles.
- 27 sts and 28 rows to 4"/10cm over color pat using larger needles.

*Take time to check gauges.*

**Note** When changing colors, twist yarns on WS to prevent holes in work.

**Cable Pat** (multiple of 6 sts plus 3)

**Row 1 (RS)** P3, *k3, p3; rep from * to end.

**Row 2** K3, *p3, k3; rep from * to end.

**Row 3** P3, *sl 1, k2, psso, p3; rep from * to end. **Row 4** K3, *p1, yo, p1, k3; rep from * to end. Rep rows 1-4 for cable pat.

### CARDIGAN—BACK

With larger needles and A, cast on 109 (119, 129, 139, 149) sts. K 3 rows.

**Beg body pat**

**Row 1 (RS)** P3, *k3, p7; rep from * to last 6 sts, k3, p3. Cont in cable pat, working p7 between cables instead of p3, for 11 rows more. **Row 12** K3, *p1, yo, p1, k2tog, k5; rep from * to last 5 sts, p1, yo, p1, k3—99 (108, 117, 126, 135) sts. **Rows 13-23** Cont in cable pat, working p6 between cables instead of p3. **Row 24** K3, *p1, yo, p1, k2tog, k4; rep from * to last 5 sts, p1, yo, p1, k3—89 (97, 105, 113, 121) sts. **Rows 25-35** Cont in cable pat, working p5 between cables instead of p3. **Row 36** K3, *p1, yo, p1, k2tog, k3; rep from * to last 5 sts, p1, yo, p1, k3—79 (86, 93, 100, 107) sts.

**Rows 37-47** Cont in cable pat, working p4 between cables instead of p3. **Row 48** K3, *p1, yo, p1, k2tog, k2; rep from * to last 5 sts, p1, yo, p1, k3—69 (75, 81, 87, 93) sts.

Cont in cable pat until piece measures 7 (7½, 8½, 9, 9½)"/17.5 (19, 21.5, 23, 24)cm from beg. Cont in St st as foll:

**Armhole shaping**

With B, bind off 7 (10, 10, 11, 14) sts at beg of next row. With A, bind off 7 (10, 10, 11, 14) sts at beg of next row—55 (55, 61, 65, 65) sts.

**Beg chart**

**Next row (RS)** Beg with row 3 of chart, work sts 22 (22, 19, 17, 17) to 24, work sts 1-24 twice, then work sts 1 to 4 (4, 7, 9, 9). Cont as established until piece measures 11 (12, 13, 14, 15)"/28 (30.5, 33, 35.5, 38)cm from beg, end with a WS row.

**Neck shaping**

**Next row (RS)** Work 15 (15, 17, 18, 18) sts, join 2nd ball of yarn and bind off center 25 (25, 27, 29, 29) sts for neck, work to end. Work both sides at once until piece measures 11½ (12½, 13½, 14½, 15½)"/29 (31.5, 34.5, 37, 39.5)cm from beg. Bind off sts each side for shoulders.

## LEFT FRONT

With larger needles and A, cast on 49 (57, 59, 62, 69) sts. K 3 rows.

**Beg body pat**

**Row 1 (RS)** P3 (2, 3, 5, 3), *k3, p7; rep from * to last 6 (5, 6, 7, 6), k3, p 3 (2, 3, 4, 3). Cont as established, working dec between cables every 12th row as for back 4 times—33 (37, 39, 42, 45) sts. Work even until same length as back through row 1 of armhole shaping—26 (27, 29, 31, 31) sts. **Next row** *P1 A, p1 C; rep from *, end p0 (1, 1, 1, 1) A.

**Beg chart**

**Next row (RS)** Beg with row 3, work sts 23 (22, 20, 18, 18) to 24, work sts 1-24 once. Cont as established until piece measures 9½ (10½, 11½, 12½, 13½)"/24 (26.5, 29, 32, 34.5)cm from beg, end with a RS row.

**Neck shaping**

**Next row (WS)** Bind off 4 (4, 5, 6, 6) sts, (neck edge) work to end. Cont to bind off from neck edge 3 sts once, 2 sts once, 1 st 2 (3, 2, 2, 2) times—15 (15, 17, 18, 18) sts. Work even until same length as back. Bind off.

## RIGHT FRONT

Work as for left front, reversing pat placement, chart and all shaping.

## SLEEVES

With smaller needles and A, cast on 33 (39, 39, 45, 45) sts. Work in k1, p1 rib for 1"/2.5cm. Change to larger needles and work in cable pat, inc 1 st each side (working inc sts into pat) every other row 11 (7, 3, 0, 3) times, then every 4th row 4 (8, 12, 15, 15) times—63 (69, 69, 75, 81) sts. Work even until piece measures 6½ (7½, 8½, 9½, 10)"/16.5 (19, 21.5, 24, 25.5)cm from beg. Bind off.

## FINISHING

Sew shoulder seams.

**Buttonband**

With RS facing, smaller needles and A, pick up and k 65 (73, 79, 85, 93) sts evenly along left front edge. Work in k1, p1 rib for ¾"/2cm. Bind off in rib. Place markers on band for two buttons, the first one 1½"/4cm from top edge and the 2nd one 2"/5cm below first one.

**Buttonhole band**

Work as for buttonband for 2 rows. Work buttonholes opposite markers on next row by working yo, k2tog for each butttonhole. Complete as for buttonband.

**Neckband**

With RS facing, smaller needles and A, pick up and k 65 (65, 69, 73, 73) sts evenly around neck edge, including top of front bands. Work in k1, p1 rib for 2 rows. Work a buttonhole as before at 3 sts in from right front edge. Work even until band measures 3/4"/2cm. Bind off in rib.

Place markers 4 3/4 (5 1/4, 5 1/4, 5 1/2, 6)"/12 (13.5, 13.5, 14, 15.5)cm down from shoulders for armholes. Sew top of sleeves between markers. Sew side and sleeve seams. Sew on buttons.

## PANTS

With smaller needles and A, cast on 53 (57, 61, 61, 65) sts. Work in k1, p1 rib for 1"/2.6cm, inc 28 (30, 32, 32, 34) sts evenly across last row—81 (87, 93, 93, 99) sts. Change to larger needles and work in cable pat, inc 1 st each side (working inc sts into pat) every 6th (6th, 6th, 8th, 8th) row 6 times—93 (99, 105, 105, 111) sts. Work even until piece measures 6 1/2 (7, 7 1/2, 8, 8 1/2)"/16.5 (17.5, 19, 20.5, 21.5)cm from beg, end with a WS row.

**Crotch shaping**

Bind off 2 sts at beg of next 4 rows. Dec 1 st each side every other row 3 times—79 (85, 91, 91, 97) sts. Work even until piece measures 4 1/2 (5, 5 1/2, 6, 6 1/2)"/11.5 (12.5, 14, 15.5, 16.5)cm above beg of crotch shaping, end with a WS row.

**Waistband ribbing**

Change to smaller needles and work in k1, p1 rib for 3"/7.5cm. Bind off in rib.

## FINISHING

Sew leg inseam from lower edge to crotch. Turn one leg inside out. Insert other leg in this leg so that RS are tog. Sew crotch seam from front to back. Turn pants right side out. Fold waist ribbing in half to WS and sew in place, leaving a small opening. Cut elastic to fit plus 1"/2.5cm. Insert elastic, overlapping ends 1/2"/1.5cm. Sew elastic. Sew opening closed.

## HAT

With smaller needles and A, cast on 101 (111, 119) sts. Work in k1, p1 rib for 4 rows. Change to larger needles.

**Beg chart**

**Next row (RS)** Work sts 23 (18, 14) to 24, work sts 1-24 for four times, then work sts 1 to 8 (8, 12). Cont as established through row 17, dec 1 (2, 1) sts on last row—100 (109, 118) sts.

**Note** You will end ready to work a WS row. From this point on, this side is referred to as RS. The brim will be turned up to RS once hat is completed.

**Beg cable pat**

**Row 1 (RS)** P4, *k3, p6; rep from * to last 6 sts, k3, p3. Cont in cable pat, working p sts between cables as established, for 10 rows more. **Row 12** K3, *p1, yo, p1, k2tog, k3; rep from * to last 5 sts, p1, yo, p1, k2tog, k1—78 (85, 92) sts. Cont in cable pat, working p sts between cables as established, for 7 rows more. **Row 20** k2tog, k1, * p1, yo, p1, k2tog, k2; rep from * to last 4 sts, p1, yo, p1, k2tog—66 (72, 78) sts. Cont in pat as established, dec 1 st between each cable as before, until there is 1 st between cables—46 (50, 54) sts. Cut yarn, leaving an end for sewing. Thread tail through rem sts and pull tightly to close opening.

## FINISHING

Sew back seam, keeping in mind that brim will be folded to RS.

**Braided tassel** (make two)

For each tassel, cut three 8"/20.5cm lengths

of A. Knot one end and braid for 3"/7.5cm. Knot other end and trim evenly. Insert one end of each tassel at center top and fasten securely to inside.

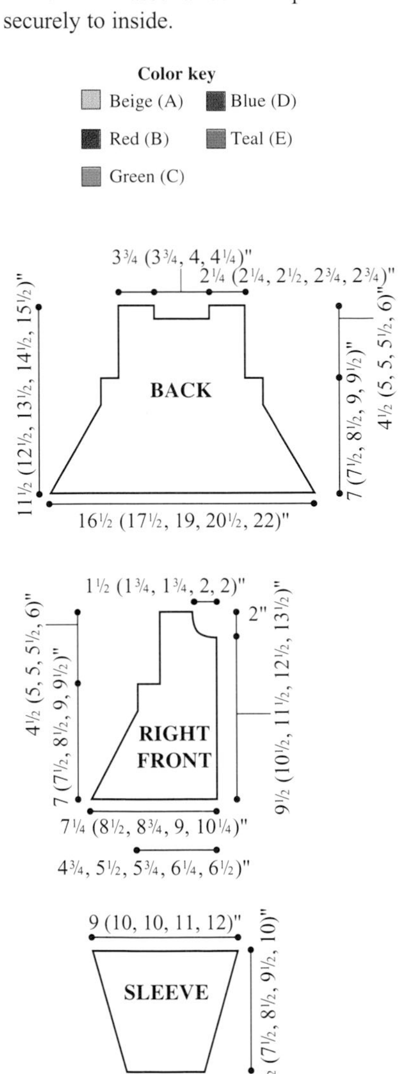


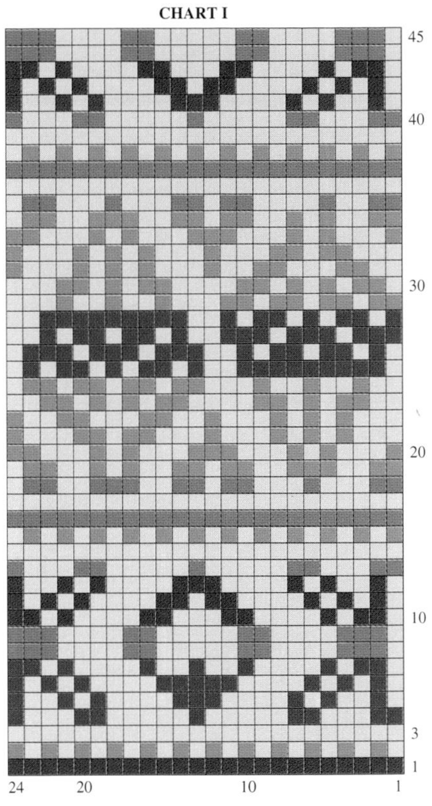


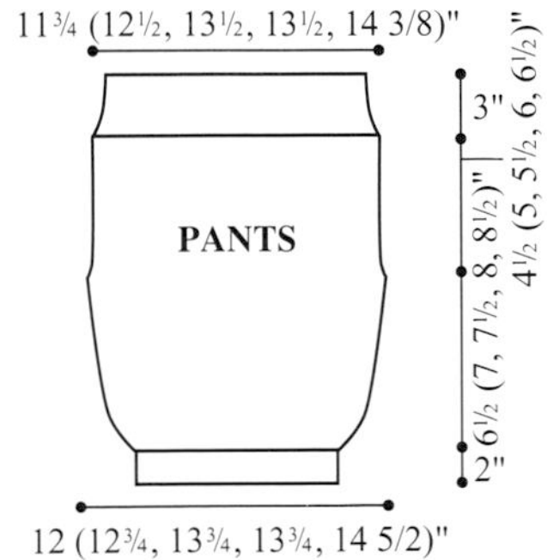

# ARAN ROMPER AND CAP

*Baby sings the blues*

*For Experienced Knitters*

**Tradition with a twist. Cuddly all-in-one has leg snaps and a back neck opening. Matching pull-on cap with pom-poms completes the set. Designed by Linda Cyr.**

### SIZES

Instructions are written for size 6 months. Changes for sizes 12, 18 and 24 months are in parentheses.

### KNITTED MEASUREMENTS

- Chest 20 (23, 24, 26)"/50 (57.5, 60, 65)cm
- Length 20¼ (25, 27½, 30)"/51.5 (63.5, 69.5, 76)cm
- Upper arm 8 (9, 10 11)"/20 (22.5, 25, 27.5)cm
- Hat circumference 15 (16, 17, 18)"/ 37.5 (40, 42.5, 45)cm

### MATERIALS

- 7 (9, 10, 12) 1¾oz/50g balls (each approx 135yd/125m) of Stahl Wolle *Limbo* (superwash wool③) in #4485 blue
- Sizes 2 and 4 (2.5 and 3.5 mm) needles, *or size to obtain gauge*
- Cable needle
- Three ½"/13mm pearl shank buttons
- Snap tape
- Stitch holder
- Size E/4 (3.5mm) crochet hook

### GAUGE

28 sts and 34 rows to 4"/10cm over moss st using larger needles.

*Take time to check gauge.*

### STITCH GLOSSARY

**Moss Stitch**

**Row 1** *K1, p1; rep from * to end. **Rows 2 and 4** K the knit and p the purl sts. **Row 3** *P1, k1; rep from * to end. Rep rows 1-4 for moss st pat.

**4-ST RC (LC)** Sl 2 to cn and hold to *back* (*front*), k2, k2 from cn.

**2-ST RC (LC)** Sl 1 to cn and hold to *back* (*front*), k1, k1 from cn.

**1/2 RPC (LPC)** Sl 1 to cn and hold to *back (front)*, k2, p1 from cn.

**2/1 LPC** Sl 2 to cn and hold to *front*, p1, k2 from cn.

**Cable panel** (over 22 sts)

**Rows 1, 5, 9, 13** P1, k4, p2, k8, p2, k4, p1. **Row 2 and all WS rows** K the knit sts and p the purl sts. **Rows 3 and 15** P1, 4-ST RC, p2, 4-ST RC, 4-ST LC, p2, 4-ST LC, p1. **Rows 7 and 11** P1, 4-ST RC, p2, 4-ST LC, 4-ST RC, p2, 4-ST LC, p1. **Row 16** Rep row 2. Rep rows 1-16 for cable panel

**Heart panel** (over 14 sts)

**Row 1** P6, k2, p6. **Rows 2, 4, 6, 8, 10, 12, and 16** K the knit sts and p the purl sts. **Row 3** P5, 2-ST RC, 2-ST LC, p5. **Row 5** P4, 1/2 RPC, 2/1 LPC, p4. **Row 7** P3, 1/2 RPC, p2, 2/1 LPC, p3. **Row 9** P2, 1/2 RPC, p4, 2/1 LPC, p2. **Row 11** [P2, k2] 3 times, p2. **Row 13** P2, 2/1 LPC, sl 1 to cn, hold in *back*, k1, p1 from cn, sl 1 to cn, hold in *front*, p1, k1 from cn, 1/2 RPC, p2. **Row 14** K3, yo, sl 2 purlwise, insert tip of LH needle into first slipped st and pass over 2nd st, replace st on LH needle, insert tip of RH needle into 2nd st on LH needle purlwise, pass over first st, k first st, yo, k2, yo, sl 1 purlwise, insert tip of RH needle purlwise into 2nd st on LH needle, pass over first st, sl onto RH needle, insert tip of LH needle into 2nd st from the end of RH needle, pass over first st, replace onto LH needle, k1, yo, k3. **Row 15** P to end. Rep rows 1-16 for heart panel.

**Right Cable** (over 5 sts)

**Rows 1 and 5 (RS)** P1, k4. **Rows 2, 4 and 6** K the knit sts and p the purl sts. **Row 3** P1, 4-st RC. Rep rows 1-6 for right cable.

**Left Cable** (over 5 sts)

**Rows 1 and 5 (RS)** K4, p1. **Rows 2, 4 and 6** K the knit sts and p the purl sts. **Row 3** 4-st LC, p1. Rep rows 1-6 for right cable.

## ROMPER FRONT

### Left leg

With smaller needles, cast on 31 (35, 37, 39) sts. Work in k1, p1 rib for 1¼"/3cm, inc 8 (8, 10, 12) sts across last row—39 (43, 47, 51) sts. Change to larger needles.

### Beg pats

**Next row (RS)** K1 (selvage st), 10 (14, 17, 19) sts moss st, 22 sts cable panel, 5 (5, 6, 8) sts moss st, k1 (selvage st). Cont as established for 3 (7, 7, 7) rows. **Next row (RS)** Work to last st, M1, k1. Cont to inc 1 st inside selvage st at end of RS rows, every 4th row 7 (9, 10, 12) times, every other row 4 (4, 4, 2) times, working incs into pats, so that final pat set up is as foll: (RS) K1, 10 (14, 17, 19) sts moss st, 22 sts cable panel, 6 (8, 10, 12) sts moss st, 5 sts right cable, p6, k1—51 (57, 62, 66) sts. Place sts on holder.

### Right leg

Work as for left leg, reversing all shaping and pat placement. Work left cable instead of right cable at shaped edge.

## BODY

**Next row (RS)** Sl left leg sts to needle with right leg sts—102 (114, 122, 132) sts. Cont as established, working center 2 sts as p2, for 2 rows. Work center 14 sts in heart panel and rem sts as established until piece measures 2¾ (3¼, 2, 2)"/7 (8, 5, 5)cm above leg joining.

### Side shaping

Dec 1 st at each side inside selvage sts on next row, then every 8th row 6 (7, 9, 11) times more—88 (98, 102, 108) sts. Work even until piece measures 8¾ (11¾, 13½, 15)"/22.5 (30, 33.5, 38)cm above leg joining.

### Armhole shaping

Bind off 3 sts at beg of next 2 rows. Work 2 rows even. Dec 1 st at each side of next row—80 (90, 94, 100) sts. Work even until armhole measures 3¼ (3¾, 4¼, 4¾)"/8 (9.5, 10.5, 12)cm.

### Neck shaping

**Next row (RS)** Work 33 (38, 40, 43) sts, join 2nd ball of yarn and bind off center 14 sts, work to end. Working both sides at once, bind off from each neck edge 4 sts 1 (2, 2, 2) times, 3 sts once, 2 sts 2 (1, 2, 3) times—22 (25, 25, 26) sts each side. Work even until armhole measures 4½ (5, 5½, 6)"/11 (12.5, 14, 15)cm, end with a RS row.

### Shoulder shaping

Bind off from each shoulder edge 8 (9, 9, 10) sts once, 7 (8, 8, 8) sts twice.

## BACK

Work as for front until piece measure 9¾ (13½, 15¼, 17¼)"/24 (34, 38, 43)cm above leg joining.

### Placket shaping

**Next row (RS)** Work 33 (38, 40, 43) sts in pat, p5, k2, join 2nd ball of yarn and p2, k5, work to end. Work both sides at once and shape as for front. Work even until same length as front to shoulder.

### Shoulder and neck shaping

Shape shoulders as for front, AT SAME TIME, bind off from each neck edge 10 (10, 12, 12) sts once, 8 (10, 10, 12) sts once.

**SLEEVES**

With smaller needles, cast on 37 (41, 45, 49) sts. Work in k1, p1 rib for 1¼"/3cm, inc 9 (11, 11, 13) sts across last row—46 (52, 56, 62) sts. Change to larger needles

**Beg pats**

**Next row (RS)** K1, work 11 (14, 16, 19) sts moss st, 22 sts cable panel, 11 (14, 16, 19) sts moss st, k1. Cont in pats as established, inc 1 st each side (working inc sts into moss st) every 4th row 4 (4, 5, 5) times, then every 8th row 3 (4, 4, 5) times—60 (68, 74, 82) sts work even piece measures 6 (7, 8, 9)"/15 (17.5, 20, 22.5)cm from beg.

**Cap shaping**

Bind off 3 sts at beg of next 2 rows, 1 st at beg of next 4 rows. Bind off rem 46 (54, 60, 72) sts.

**FINISHING**

Block pieces. Sew shoulder seams.

**Collar**

With RS facing and smaller needles, pick up and k 99 (102, 105, 107) sts around neck edge. Work in k1, p1 rib for ¾"/2cm. Bind off, do not cut yarn. Place markers for buttons on left side of placket with top button at base of collar. With crochet hook, sc along sides of placket, making a ch-10 button lp opposite markers. Sew on buttons.

**Leg bands**

With RS facing and smaller needles, pick up and k 88 (104, 112, 120) sts across front leg opening, excluding rib. Work in k1, p1 rib for ½"/1.5cm. Bind off in rib. Rep for back leg opening. Cut 2 pieces snap tape plus 1"/2.5cm. Fold under ½"/1.5cm on each end of snap tape and sew to WS of leg bands. Fold leg bands to inside. Sew leg cuff seams. Sew side and underarm seams.

**HAT**

(make 2 pieces)

With smaller needles, cast on 64 (68, 72, 76) sts. Work in k1, p1 rib for 1¼"/3cm, end WS row. Change to larger needles.

**Beg pats**

**Next row (RS)** K1 (selvage st), work 2 (4, 6, 8) sts moss st, 22 sts cable panel (change last cable to right cable), 14 sts heart panel, 22 sts cable panel (change first cable to left cable), 2 (4, 6, 8) sts moss st, k1 (selvage st). Cont in pat as established until piece measures 5 (5, 7, 7)"/12.5 (12.5, 17.5, 17.5)cm from beg. Bind off all sts.

**FINISHING**

Lightly block pieces. Sew side and top seams. Make two 1½"/4cm pom-poms (see template, page 64), sew to corners.

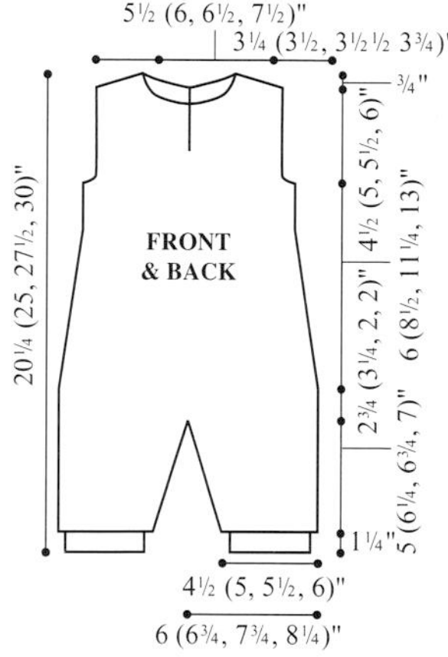


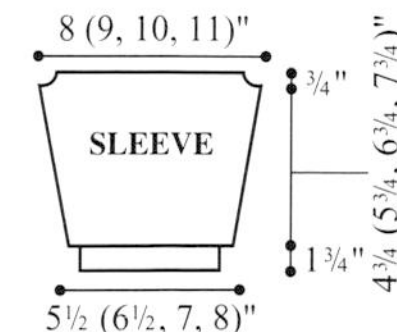

# RESOURCES

## US RESOURCES

*Write to the yarn companies listed below for purchasing and mail-order information.*

**AD HOC**
distributed by
Stacy Charles Collection

**ANGUS INTERNATIONAL**
55 West 39th Street
New York, NY 10018

**BARUFFA**
distributed by Lane Borgosesia

**BERROCO, INC.**
14 Elmdale Road
PO Box 367
Uxbridge, MA 01569

**BROWN SHEEP CO., INC.**
100662 County Road 16
Mitchell, NE 69357

**CLASSIC ELITE YARNS**
12 Perkins Street
Lowell, MA 01854

**CLECKHEATON**
distributed by Plymouth Yarn

**COLINETTE YARNS, LTD.**
distributed by Unique Kolours

**DALE OF NORWAY, INC.**
N16 W23390 Stoneridge Drive
Suite A
Waukesha, WI 53188

**DARICE, INC.**
21160 Drake Road
Strongsville, OH 44136
(440) 238-9150

**FILATURA DI CROSA**
distributed by
Stacy Charles Collection

**KOIGU WOOL DESIGNS**
R.R. #1
Williamsford, ON
N0H 2V0
Canada

**JCA**
35 Scales Lane
Townsend, MA 01469

**JHB BUTTONS**
JHB International, Inc.
(303) 751-8100

**LANE BORGOSESIA**
PO Box 217
Colorado Springs, CO 80903

**LANG**
distributed by
Berroco, Inc.

**LION BRAND YARN**
34 West 15th Street
New York, NY 10011
www.lionbrand.com

**ONE WORLD BUTTON SUPPLY CO.**
41 Union Square West
Room 311
New York, NY 10003

**PINGOUIN**
distributed by
Lane Borgosesia

**PLYMOUTH YARN**
PO Box 28
Bristol, PA 19007

**REYNOLDS**
distributed by JCA

**ROWAN**
distributed by
Westminster Fibers

**SCHAFFHAUSER**
distributed by
Skacel Collection

**SKACEL COLLECTION**
PO Box 88110
Seattle, WA 98138-2110

**SPINRITE YARNS, LTD.**
PO Box 40
Listowel, ON N4W 3H3
Canada

**STACY CHARLES COLLECTION**
1059/1061 Manhattan Avenue
Brooklyn, NY 11222

**STAHL WOLLE**
distributed by
Tahki Imports, Ltd.

**TAHKI IMPORTS, LTD.**
11 Graphic Place
Moonachie, NJ 07074

**TRENDSETTER YARNS**
16742 Stagg Street
Suite 104
Van Nuys, CA 91406

**UNIQUE KOLOURS**
1428 Oak Lane
Downingtown, PA. 19335

**WESTMINSTER FIBERS**
5 Northern Boulevard
Amherst, NH 03031

## CANADIAN RESOURCES

*Write to US resources for mail-order availability of yarns not listed.*

**CLASSIC ELITE YARNS**
distributed by
S. R. Kertzer, Ltd.

**CLECKHEATON**
distributed by Diamond Yarn

**COLINETTE YARNS, LTD.**
distributed by Diamond Yarn

**DIAMOND YARN**
9697 St. Laurent
Montreal, PQ H3L 2N1
*and* 1450 Lodestar Road
Unit #4
Toronto, ON M3J 3C1

**FILATURA DI CROSA**
distributed by
Diamond Yarn

**S. R. KERTZER, LTD.**
105A Winges Road
Woodbridge, ON L4L 6C2

**KOIGU WOOL DESIGNS**
R.R. #1
Williamsford, ON N0H 2V0

**LANG**
distributed by
R. Stein Yarn Corp.

**PINGOUIN**
distributed by
Promafil Canada Ltee.

**PROMAFIL CANADA LTEE.**
300 Marcel Laurin
Suite 100
St. Laurent, PQ H4M 2L4

**R. STEIN YARN CORP.**
5800 St. Denis
Suite 303
Montreal, PQ H2S 3L5

**ROWAN**
distributed by Diamond Yarn

**SPINRITE, LTD.**
PO Box 40
Listowel, ON N4W 3H3

**STAHL WOLLE**
distributed by
Diamond Yarn

---

## UK RESOURCES

*Not all yarns used in this book are available in the UK. For yarns not available, make a comparable substitute or contact the US manufacturer for purchasing and mail-order information.*

*In the UK, Cleckheaton is sold as Jarol Super Saver DK*

**JAROL, LTD.**
White Rose Mills
Cape Street
Canal Road
Bradford, BD1 4RN
Tel: 0274-392274

**COLINETTE YARNS, LTD.**
Units 2-5
Banwy Industrial Estate
Llanfair Caereinion
Powys SY21 OSG
Tel: 02938-810128

**PINGOUIN**
Pingouin Carlisle
20 Globe Lane
Carlisle CA3 8NX
Tel: 01228 520681

**ROWAN YARNS**
Green Lane Mill
Holmfirth
West Yorks HD7 1RW
Tel: 01484-681881

# VOGUE KNITTING BABY KNITS

Editor-in-Chief
**TRISHA MALCOLM**

Art Director, Butterick® Company, Inc
**JOE VIOR**

Book Designer
**CHRISTINE LIPERT**

Senior Editor
**CARLA S. SCOTT**

Managing Editor
**DARYL BROWER**

Knitting Coordinator
**JEAN GUIRGUIS**

Yarn Coordinator
**VERONICA MANNO**

Charts & Schematics Illustrator/
Page Layout
**ELIZABETH BERRY**

Instructions Coordinator
**CHARLOTTE PARRY**

Editorial Coordinator
**KATHLEEN KELLY**

Photography
**BRIAN KRAUS, NYC**
Photographed at Butterick Studios

Project Director
**CAROLINE POLITI**

Production Managers
**LILLIAN ESPOSITO**
**WINNIE HINISH**

Publishing Consultant
**MIKE SHATZKIN, THE IDEALOGICAL COMPANY**

■

President and CEO, Butterick® Company, Inc
**JAY H. STEIN**

Executive Vice President and Publisher, Butterick® Company, Inc
**ART JOINNIDES**